BAHÁ'Í PRAYERS

A SELECTION OF PRAYERS
REVEALED BY
BAHÁ'U'LLÁH, THE BÁB, AND 'ABDU'L-BAHÁ

*Blessed is the spot, and the house,
and the place, and the city,
and the heart, and the mountain,
and the refuge, and the cave,
and the valley, and the land,
and the sea, and the island,
and the meadow where mention
of God hath been made,
and His praise glorified.*

—*BAHÁ'U'LLÁH*

Bahá'í Publishing Trust

WILMETTE, ILLINOIS 60091

Bahá'í Publishing Trust
415 Linden Avenue, Wilmette, IL 60091-2886
Copyright 1954, © 1982, 1985, 1991, 2002 by the
National Spiritual Assembly of the
Bahá'ís of the United States
2002 Edition
All Rights Reserved

Reprinted 2013

The Library of Congress has cataloged the softcover edition as follows:
Bahá'u'lláh, 1817–1892.
    [Prayers. English. Selections]
    Bahá'í prayers : a selection of prayers / revealed by
Bahá'u'lláh, the Báb, and 'Abdu'l-Bahá.
        p.   cm.
Includes index.
ISBN 0-87743-285-6 (alk. paper)
  1. Bahai Faith—Prayer-books and devotions—English.
I. Bab, 'Ali Muhammad Shirazi, 1819–1850. II. 'Abdu'l-Bahá,
1844–1921. III. Title.

BP360 .B12 2002
297.9'3433—dc21

2002037581

Printed in China on acid-free paper ∞

978-0-87743-344-6 (softcover)
978-0-87743-345-3 (hardcover)
978-0-87743-346-0 (leather)

Intone, O My servant, the verses of God
    that have been received by thee,
as intoned by them who have drawn
    nigh unto Him,
that the sweetness of thy melody
    may kindle thine own soul,
and attract the hearts of all men.
    Whoso reciteth, in the privacy of his chamber,
the verses revealed by God,
    the scattering angels of the Almighty
shall scatter abroad the fragrance
    of the words uttered by his mouth,
and shall cause the heart
    of every righteous man to throb.
Though he may, at first, remain unaware
    of its effect, yet the virtue
of the grace vouchsafed unto him
    must needs sooner or later exercise
its influence upon his soul.
    Thus have the mysteries of the Revelation
of God been decreed
    by virtue of the Will of Him
Who is the Source of power and wisdom.
                              —BAHÁ'U'LLÁH

CONTENTS

The headings designated are purely arbitrary,
for the purpose of easier location of the prayers,
and are not a part of the sacred texts.

v

CONTENTS

OBLIGATORY PRAYERS

OBLIGATORY PRAYERS

"The daily obligatory prayers are three in number. . . . The believer is entirely free to choose any one of these three prayers, but is under the obligation of reciting one of them, and in accordance with any specific directions with which it may be accompanied."—from a letter written on behalf of Shoghi Effendi

"By 'morning,' 'noon' and 'evening,' mentioned in connection with the Obligatory Prayers, is meant respectively the intervals between sunrise and noon, between noon and sunset, and from sunset till two hours after sunset." —Synopsis and Codification of the Kitáb-i-Aqdas, p. 36

SHORT OBLIGATORY PRAYER

TO BE RECITED ONCE IN TWENTY-FOUR HOURS,
AT NOON

I bear witness, O my God, that Thou hast created me to know Thee and to worship Thee. I testify, at this moment, to my powerlessness and to Thy might, to my poverty and to Thy wealth.

There is none other God but Thee, the Help in Peril, the Self-Subsisting. —*Bahá'u'lláh*

MEDIUM OBLIGATORY PRAYER

TO BE RECITED DAILY, IN THE MORNING,
AT NOON, AND IN THE EVENING

Whoso wisheth to pray, let him wash his hands, and while he washeth, let him say:

Strengthen my hand, O my God, that it may take hold of Thy Book with such steadfastness that the hosts of the world shall have no power over it. Guard it, then, from meddling with whatsoever doth not belong unto it. Thou art, verily, the Almighty, the Most Powerful.

And while washing his face, let him say:

I have turned my face unto Thee, O my Lord! Illumine it with the light of Thy countenance. Protect it, then, from turning to anyone but Thee.

Then let him stand up, and facing the Qiblih (Point of Adoration, i.e., Bahjí, 'Akká), let him say:

God testifieth that there is none other God but Him. His are the kingdoms of Revelation and of creation. He, in truth, hath manifested Him Who is the Dayspring of Revelation, Who conversed on Sinai, through Whom the Supreme Horizon hath been made to shine, and the Lote-Tree beyond which there is no passing hath spoken, and through Whom the call hath been proclaimed unto all who are in heaven and on earth: "Lo, the All-Possessing is come. Earth and heaven, glory and dominion are God's, the Lord of all men, and the Possessor of the Throne on high and of earth below!"

Let him, then, bend down, with hands resting on the knees, and say:

Exalted art Thou above my praise and the praise of anyone beside me, above my description and the description of all who are in heaven and all who are on earth!

Then, standing with open hands, palms upward toward the face, let him say:

Disappoint not, O my God, him that hath, with beseeching fingers, clung to the hem of Thy mercy and Thy grace, O Thou Who of those who show mercy art the Most Merciful!

Let him, then, be seated and say:

I bear witness to Thy unity and Thy oneness, and that Thou art God, and that there is none other God beside Thee. Thou hast, verily, revealed Thy Cause, fulfilled Thy Covenant, and opened wide the door of Thy grace to all that dwell in heaven and on earth. Blessing and peace, salutation and glory, rest upon Thy loved ones, whom the changes and chances of the world have not deterred from turning unto Thee, and who have given their all, in the hope of obtaining that which is with Thee. Thou art, in truth, the Ever-Forgiving, the All-Bountiful.

> *(If anyone choose to recite instead of the long verse these words: "God testifieth that there is none other God but Him, the Help in Peril, the Self-Subsisting," it would be sufficient. And likewise, it would suffice were he, while seated, to choose to recite these words: "I bear witness to Thy unity and Thy oneness, and that Thou art God, and that there is none other God beside Thee.")*
>
> —*Bahá'u'lláh*

LONG OBLIGATORY PRAYER

TO BE RECITED ONCE IN TWENTY-FOUR HOURS

> *Whoso wisheth to recite this prayer, let him stand up and turn unto God, and, as he standeth in his place, let him gaze to the right and to the left, as if awaiting the mercy of his Lord, the Most Merciful, the Compassionate. Then let him say:*

O Thou Who art the Lord of all names and the Maker of the heavens! I beseech Thee by them Who are the Daysprings of Thine invisible Essence, the Most Exalted,

the All-Glorious, to make of my prayer a fire
that will burn away the veils which have shut
me out from Thy beauty, and a light that will
lead me unto the ocean of Thy Presence.

*Let him then raise his hands in supplication toward
God—blessed and exalted be He—and say:*

O Thou the Desire of the world and the Beloved of the nations! Thou seest me turning
toward Thee, and rid of all attachment to anyone save Thee, and clinging to Thy cord,
through whose movement the whole creation
hath been stirred up. I am Thy servant, O my
Lord, and the son of Thy servant. Behold me
standing ready to do Thy will and Thy desire,
and wishing naught else except Thy good pleasure. I implore Thee by the Ocean of Thy
mercy and the Daystar of Thy grace to do with
Thy servant as Thou willest and pleasest. By
Thy might which is far above all mention and
praise! Whatsoever is revealed by Thee is the
desire of my heart and the beloved of my soul.
O God, my God! Look not upon my hopes and
my doings, nay rather look upon Thy will that

hath encompassed the heavens and the earth. By Thy Most Great Name, O Thou Lord of all nations! I have desired only what Thou didst desire, and love only what Thou dost love.

Let him then kneel, and bowing his forehead to the ground, let him say:

Exalted art Thou above the description of anyone save Thyself, and the comprehension of aught else except Thee.

Let him then stand and say:

Make my prayer, O my Lord, a fountain of living waters whereby I may live as long as Thy sovereignty endureth, and may make mention of Thee in every world of Thy worlds.

Let him again raise his hands in supplication, and say:

O Thou in separation from Whom hearts and souls have melted, and by the fire of Whose love the whole world hath been set aflame! I implore Thee by Thy Name through which Thou hast subdued the whole creation, not to withhold from me that which is with Thee, O Thou Who rulest over all men! Thou seest, O my Lord, this stranger hastening to his most exalted home beneath the canopy of Thy majesty and within the precincts of Thy mercy; and this transgressor seeking the ocean of Thy forgiveness; and this lowly one the court of Thy glory; and this poor creature the orient of Thy wealth. Thine is the authority to command whatsoever Thou willest. I bear witness that Thou art to be praised in Thy doings, and to be obeyed in Thy behests, and to remain unconstrained in Thy bidding.

Let him then raise his hands, and repeat three times the Greatest Name.* Let him then bend down with hands resting on the knees before God—blessed and exalted be He—and say:

Thou seest, O my God, how my spirit hath been stirred up within my limbs and members, in its longing to worship Thee, and in its yearning to remember Thee and extol Thee; how it

---

* Alláh-u-Abhá.

testifieth to that whereunto the Tongue of Thy Commandment hath testified in the kingdom of Thine utterance and the heaven of Thy knowledge. I love, in this state, O my Lord to beg of Thee all that is with Thee, that I may demonstrate my poverty, and magnify Thy bounty and Thy riches, and may declare my powerlessness, and manifest Thy power and Thy might.

Let him then stand and raise his hands twice in supplication, and say:

There is no God but Thee, the Almighty, the All-Bountiful. There is no God but Thee, the Ordainer, both in the beginning and in the end. O God, my God! Thy forgiveness hath emboldened me, and Thy mercy hath strengthened me, and Thy call hath awakened me, and Thy grace hath raised me up and led me unto Thee. Who, otherwise, am I that I should dare to stand at the gate of the city of Thy nearness, or set my face toward the lights that are shining from the heaven of Thy will? Thou seest, O my Lord, this wretched creature knocking at the door of Thy grace, and this evanescent soul seeking the river of everlasting life from the hands of Thy bounty. Thine is the command at all times, O Thou Who art the Lord of all names; and mine is resignation and willing submission to Thy will, O Creator of the heavens!

Let him then raise his hands thrice, and say:

Greater is God than every great one!

Let him then kneel and, bowing his forehead to the ground, say:

Too high art Thou for the praise of those who are nigh unto Thee to ascend unto the heaven of Thy nearness, or for the birds of the hearts of them who are devoted to Thee to attain to the door of Thy gate. I testify that Thou hast been sanctified above all attributes and holy above all names. No God is there but Thee, the Most Exalted, the All-Glorious.

Let him then seat himself and say:

I testify unto that whereunto have testified all created things, and the Concourse on high, and the inmates of the all-highest Paradise, and beyond them the Tongue of Grandeur itself from the all-glorious Horizon, that Thou art God, that there is no God but Thee, and that He Who hath been manifested is the Hidden Mystery, the Treasured Symbol, through Whom the letters B and E (Be) have been joined and knit together. I testify that it is He Whose name hath been set down by the Pen of the Most High, and Who hath been mentioned in the Books of God, the Lord of the Throne on high and of earth below.

Let him then stand erect and say:

O Lord of all being and Possessor of all things visible and invisible! Thou dost perceive my tears and the sighs I utter, and hearest my groaning, and my wailing, and the lamentation of my heart. By Thy might! My trespasses have kept me back from drawing nigh unto Thee; and my sins have held me far from the court of Thy holiness. Thy love, O my Lord, hath enriched me, and separation from Thee hath destroyed me, and remoteness from Thee hath consumed me. I entreat Thee by Thy footsteps in this wilderness, and by the words "Here am I. Here am I," which Thy chosen Ones have uttered in this immensity, and by the breaths of Thy Revelation, and the gentle winds of the Dawn of Thy Manifestation, to ordain that I may gaze on Thy beauty and observe whatsoever is in Thy Book.

Let him then repeat the Greatest Name thrice, and bend down with hands resting on the knees, and say:

Praise be to Thee, O my God, that Thou hast aided me to remember Thee and to praise Thee, and hast made known unto me Him Who is the Dayspring of Thy signs, and hast caused me to bow down before Thy Lordship, and humble myself before Thy Godhead, and to acknowledge that which hath been uttered by the Tongue of Thy grandeur.

Let him then rise and say:

O God, my God! My back is bowed by the burden of my sins, and my heedlessness hath destroyed me. Whenever I ponder my evil doings and Thy benevolence, my heart melteth within me, and my blood boileth in my veins. By Thy Beauty, O Thou the Desire of the world! I blush to lift up my face to Thee, and my longing hands are ashamed to stretch forth toward the heaven of Thy bounty. Thou seest, O my God, how my tears prevent me from remembering Thee and from extolling Thy virtues, O Thou the Lord of the Throne on high and of earth below! I implore Thee by the signs of Thy Kingdom and the mysteries of Thy Dominion to do with Thy loved ones as becometh Thy bounty, O Lord of all being, and is worthy of Thy grace, O King of the seen and the unseen!

Let him then repeat the Greatest Name thrice, and kneel with his forehead to the ground, and say:

Praise be unto Thee, O our God, that Thou hast sent down unto us that which draweth us nigh unto Thee, and supplieth us with every good thing sent down by Thee in Thy Books and Thy Scriptures. Protect us, we beseech Thee, O my Lord, from the hosts of idle fancies and vain imaginations. Thou, in truth, art the Mighty, the All-Knowing.

Let him then raise his head, and seat himself, and say:

I testify, O my God, to that whereunto Thy chosen Ones have testified, and acknowledge that which the inmates of the all-highest Paradise and those who have circled round Thy mighty Throne have acknowledged. The kingdoms of earth and heaven are Thine, O Lord of the worlds!   —*Bahá'u'lláh*

GENERAL PRAYERS

AID AND ASSISTANCE

O Thou Whose face is the object of my adoration, Whose beauty is my sanctuary, Whose habitation is my goal, Whose praise is my hope, Whose providence is my companion, Whose love is the cause of my being, Whose mention is my solace, Whose nearness is my desire, Whose presence is my dearest wish and highest aspiration, I entreat Thee not to withhold from me the things Thou didst ordain for the chosen ones among Thy servants. Supply me, then, with the good of this world and of the next.

Thou, truly, art the King of all men. There is no God but Thee, the Ever-Forgiving, the Most Generous.   —*Bahá'u'lláh*

M y God, my Adored One, my King, my Desire! What tongue can voice my thanks to Thee? I was heedless, Thou didst awaken me. I had turned back from Thee, Thou didst graciously aid me to turn towards Thee. I was as one dead, Thou didst quicken me with the water of life. I was withered, Thou didst revive me with the heavenly stream of Thine utterance which hath flowed forth from the Pen of the All-Merciful.

O Divine Providence! All existence is begotten by Thy bounty; deprive it not of the waters of Thy generosity, neither do Thou withhold it from the ocean of Thy mercy. I beseech Thee to aid and assist me at all times and under all conditions, and seek from the heaven of Thy grace Thine ancient favor. Thou art, in truth, the Lord of bounty, and the Sovereign of the kingdom of eternity.   —*Bahá'u'lláh*

Lauded be Thy Name, O Lord our God! Thou art in truth the Knower of things unseen. Ordain for us such good as Thine all-embracing knowledge can measure. Thou art the sovereign Lord, the Almighty, the Best-Beloved.

All praise be unto Thee, O Lord! We shall

seek Thy grace on the appointed Day and shall put our whole reliance in Thee, Who art our Lord. Glorified art Thou, O God! Grant us that which is good and seemly that we may be able to dispense with everything but Thee. Verily, Thou art the Lord of all worlds.

O God! Recompense those who endure patiently in Thy days, and strengthen their hearts to walk undeviatingly in the path of Truth. Grant then, O Lord, such goodly gifts as would enable them to gain admittance into Thy blissful Paradise. Exalted art Thou, O Lord God. Let Thy heavenly blessings descend upon homes whose inmates have believed in Thee. Verily, unsurpassed art Thou in sending down divine blessings. Send forth, O God, such hosts as would render Thy faithful servants victorious. Thou dost fashion the created things through the power of Thy decree as Thou pleasest. Thou art in truth the Sovereign, the Creator, the All-Wise.

Say: God is indeed the Maker of all things. He giveth sustenance in plenty to whomsoever He willeth. He is the Creator, the Source of all beings, the Fashioner, the Almighty, the Maker,

the All-Wise. He is the Bearer of the most excellent titles throughout the heavens and the
earth and whatever lieth between them. All do
His bidding, and all the dwellers of earth and
heaven celebrate His praise, and unto Him shall
all return.   —*The Báb*

O my God, my Lord and my Master! I
have detached myself from my kindred
and have sought through Thee to become independent of all that dwell on earth and ever
ready to receive that which is praiseworthy in
Thy sight. Bestow on me such good as will
make me independent of aught else but
Thee, and grant me an ampler share of Thy
boundless favors. Verily, Thou art the Lord
of grace abounding.   —*The Báb*

Lord! Pitiful are we, grant us Thy favor;
poor, bestow upon us a share from the
ocean of Thy wealth; needy, do Thou satisfy
us; abased, give us Thy glory. The fowls of
the air and the beasts of the field receive their
meat each day from Thee, and all beings partake of Thy care and loving-kindness.

Deprive not this feeble one of Thy wondrous grace and vouchsafe by Thy might unto this helpless soul Thy bounty.

Give us our daily bread, and grant Thine increase in the necessities of life, that we may be dependent on none other but Thee, may commune wholly with Thee, may walk in Thy ways and declare Thy mysteries. Thou art the Almighty and the Loving and the Provider of all mankind.   —'Abdu'l-Bahá

O Thou kind Lord! We are servants of Thy Threshold, taking shelter at Thy holy Door. We seek no refuge save only this strong pillar, turn nowhere for a haven but unto Thy safekeeping. Protect us, bless us, support us, make us such that we shall love but Thy good pleasure, utter only Thy praise, follow only the pathway of truth, that we may become rich enough to dispense with all save Thee, and receive our gifts from the sea of Thy beneficence, that we may ever strive to exalt Thy Cause and to spread Thy sweet savors far and wide, that we may become oblivious of self and occupied only with Thee, and disown all else and be caught up in Thee.

O Thou Provider, O Thou Forgiver! Grant us Thy grace and loving-kindness, Thy gifts and Thy bestowals, and sustain us, that we may attain our goal. Thou art the Powerful, the Able, the Knower, the Seer; and, verily, Thou art the Generous, and, verily, Thou art the All-Merciful, and, verily, Thou art the Ever-Forgiving, He to Whom repentance is due, He Who forgiveth even the most grievous of sins.

—'Abdu'l-Bahá

Remove not, O Lord, the festal board that hath been spread in Thy Name, and extinguish not the burning flame that hath been kindled by Thine unquenchable fire. Withhold not from flowing that living water of Thine that murmureth with the melody of Thy glory and Thy remembrance, and deprive not Thy servants from the fragrance of Thy sweet savors breathing forth the perfume of Thy love.

Lord! Turn the distressing cares of Thy holy ones into ease, their hardship into comfort, their abasement into glory, their sorrow into blissful joy, O Thou that holdest in Thy grasp the reins of all mankind!

Thou art, verily, the One, the Single, the Mighty, the All-Knowing, the All-Wise.

—'Abdu'l-Bahá

AMERICA

O Thou kind Lord! This gathering is turning to Thee. These hearts are radiant with Thy love. These minds and spirits are exhilarated by the message of Thy glad-tidings. O God! Let this American democracy become glorious in spiritual degrees even as it has aspired to material degrees, and render this just government victorious. Confirm this revered nation to upraise the standard of the oneness of humanity, to promulgate the Most Great Peace, to become thereby most glorious and praiseworthy among all the nations of the world. O God! This American nation is worthy of Thy favors and is deserving of Thy mercy. Make it precious and near to Thee through Thy bounty and bestowal.

—'Abdu'l-Bahá

CHILDREN

O Lord, my God! This is a child that hath sprung from the loins of one of Thy servants to whom Thou hast granted a distinguished station in the Tablets of Thine irrevocable decree in the Books of Thy behest.

I beseech Thee by Thy name, whereby everyone is enabled to attain the object of his desire, to grant that this child may become a more mature soul amongst Thy servants; cause him to shine forth through the power of Thy name, enable him to utter Thy praise, to set his face towards Thee and to draw nigh unto Thee. Verily, it is Thou Who hast, from everlasting, been powerful to do as Thou willest and Who wilt, to eternity, remain potent to do as Thou pleasest. There is none other God but Thee, the Exalted, the August, the Subduer, the Mighty, the All-Compelling.

—*Bahá'u'lláh*

O God! Educate these children. These children are the plants of Thine orchard, the flowers of Thy meadow, the roses of Thy garden. Let Thy rain fall upon them; let the Sun of Reality shine upon them with Thy love. Let Thy breeze refresh them in order that they may be trained, grow and develop, and appear in the utmost beauty. Thou art the Giver. Thou art the Compassionate.   —'Abdu'l-Bahá

O Thou kind Lord! These lovely children are the handiwork of the fingers of Thy might and the wondrous signs of Thy greatness. O God! Protect these children, graciously assist them to be educated and enable them to render service to the world of humanity. O God! These children are pearls, cause them to be nurtured within the shell of Thy loving-kindness.

Thou art the Bountiful, the All-Loving.
                    —'Abdu'l-Bahá

O Lord! Make these children excellent plants. Let them grow and develop in the Garden of Thy Covenant, and bestow freshness and beauty through the outpourings from the clouds of the all-glorious Kingdom.

O Thou kind Lord! I am a little child, exalt me by admitting me to the kingdom. I am earthly, make me heavenly; I am of the world below, let me belong to the realm above; gloomy, suffer me to become radiant; material, make me spiritual, and grant that I may manifest Thine infinite bounties.

Thou art the Powerful, the All-Loving.

—'Abdu'l-Bahá

He is God! O God, my God! Bestow upon me a pure heart, like unto a pearl.

—'Abdu'l-Bahá

O God, guide me, protect me, make of me a shining lamp and a brilliant star. Thou art the Mighty and the Powerful.

—'Abdu'l-Bahá

O my Lord! O my Lord!
I am a child of tender years. Nourish me

from the breast of Thy mercy, train me in the
bosom of Thy love, educate me in the school
of Thy guidance and develop me under the
shadow of Thy bounty. Deliver me from darkness, make me a brilliant light; free me from
unhappiness, make me a flower of the rose garden; suffer me to become a servant of Thy
threshold and confer upon me the disposition
and nature of the righteous; make me a cause
of bounty to the human world, and crown my
head with the diadem of eternal life.

Verily, Thou art the Powerful, the Mighty,
the Seer, the Hearer.   —'Abdu'l-Bahá

O Peerless Lord! Be Thou a shelter for this
poor child and a kind and forgiving
Master unto this erring and unhappy soul. O
Lord! Though we are but worthless plants,
yet we belong to Thy garden of roses.
Though saplings without leaves and blossoms, yet we are a part of Thine orchard.
Nurture this plant then through the outpourings of the clouds of Thy tender mercy
and quicken and refresh this sapling through
the reviving breath of Thy spiritual spring-

time. Suffer him to become heedful, discerning and noble, and grant that he may attain eternal life and abide in Thy Kingdom for evermore.

— *'Abdu'l-Bahá*

O my God! O my God! Thou seest these children who are the twigs of the tree of life, the birds of the meads of salvation, the pearls of the ocean of Thy grace, the roses of the garden of Thy guidance.

O God, our Lord! We sing Thy praise, bear witness to Thy sanctity and implore fervently the heaven of Thy mercy to make us lights of guidance, stars shining above the horizons of eternal glory amongst mankind, and to teach us a knowledge which proceedeth from Thee. Yá Bahá'u'l-Abhá!

— *'Abdu'l-Bahá*

O Lord! I am a child; enable me to grow beneath the shadow of Thy loving-kindness. I am a tender plant; cause me to be nurtured through the outpourings of the clouds of Thy bounty. I am a sapling of the garden of love; make me into a fruitful tree.

Thou art the Mighty and the Powerful, and

Thou art the All-Loving, the All-Knowing, the All-Seeing.   —'Abdu'l-Bahá

O Thou most glorious Lord! Make this little maidservant of Thine blessed and happy; cause her to be cherished at the threshold of Thy oneness, and let her drink deep from the cup of Thy love so that she may be filled with rapture and ecstasy and diffuse sweet-scented fragrance. Thou art the Mighty and the Powerful, and Thou art the All-Knowing, the All-Seeing.

—'Abdu'l-Bahá

INFANTS

Praised be Thou, O Lord my God! Graciously grant that this infant be fed from the breast of Thy tender mercy and loving providence and be nourished with the fruit of Thy celestial trees. Suffer him not to be committed to the care of anyone save Thee, inasmuch as Thou, Thyself, through the potency of Thy sovereign will and power, didst

create and call him into being. There is none
other God but Thee, the Almighty, the All-
Knowing.

Lauded art Thou, O my Best Beloved, waft
over him the sweet savors of Thy transcendent
bounty and the fragrances of Thy holy bestowals. Enable him then to seek shelter beneath
the shadow of Thy most exalted Name, O
Thou Who holdest in Thy grasp the kingdom
of names and attributes. Verily, Thou art potent to do what Thou willest, and Thou art
indeed the Mighty, the Exalted, the Ever-Forgiving, the Gracious, the Generous, the Merciful. — *Bahá'u'lláh*

O Thou peerless Lord! Let this suckling
babe be nursed from the breast of Thy
loving-kindness, guard it within the cradle of
Thy safety and protection and grant that it
be reared in the arms of Thy tender affection.
— *'Abdu'l-Bahá*

O God! Rear this little babe in the bosom
of Thy love, and give it milk from the
breast of Thy Providence. Cultivate this fresh

plant in the rose garden of Thy love and aid it to grow through the showers of Thy bounty. Make it a child of the kingdom, and lead it to Thy heavenly realm. Thou art powerful and kind, and Thou art the Bestower, the Generous, the Lord of surpassing bounty.

— *'Abdu'l-Bahá*

THE DEPARTED

PRAYER FOR THE DEAD

(The Prayer for the Dead is the only Bahá'í obligatory
prayer that is to be recited in congregation; it is to be
recited by one believer while all present stand in si-
lence. Bahá'u'lláh has clarified that this prayer is re-
quired only when the deceased is over the age of fifteen,
that its recital must precede interment, and that there
is no requirement to face the Qiblih during its recita-
tion. "Alláh-u-Abhá" is said once; then the first of the
six verses is recited nineteen times. Then "Alláh-u-
Abhá" is said again, followed by the second verse,
which is recited nineteen times, and so on.)

O my God! This is Thy servant and the
son of Thy servant who hath believed in
Thee and in Thy signs, and set his face towards Thee, wholly detached from all except
Thee. Thou art, verily, of those who show
mercy the most merciful.

Deal with him, O Thou Who forgivest the sins of men and concealest their faults, as beseemeth the heaven of Thy bounty and the ocean of Thy grace. Grant him admission within the precincts of Thy transcendent mercy that was before the foundation of earth and heaven. There is no God but Thee, the Ever-Forgiving, the Most Generous.

Let him, then, repeat six times the greeting "Alláh-u-Abhá," and then repeat nineteen times each of the following verses:

We all, verily, worship God.
We all, verily, bow down before God.
We all, verily, are devoted unto God.
We all, verily, give praise unto God.
We all, verily, yield thanks unto God.
We all, verily, are patient in God.

(If the dead be a woman, let him say: This is Thy handmaiden and the daughter of Thy handmaiden, etc. . . .)

—*Bahá'u'lláh*

GENERAL PRAYERS
FOR THE DEPARTED

Glory be to Thee, O Lord my God! Abase not him whom Thou hast exalted through the power of Thine everlasting sovereignty, and remove not far from Thee him whom Thou hast caused to enter the tabernacle of Thine eternity. Wilt Thou cast away, O my God, him whom Thou hast overshadowed with Thy Lordship, and wilt Thou turn away from Thee, O my Desire, him to whom Thou hast been a refuge? Canst Thou degrade him whom Thou hast uplifted, or forget him whom Thou didst enable to remember Thee?

Glorified, immensely glorified art Thou! Thou art He Who from everlasting hath been the King of the entire creation and its Prime Mover, and Thou wilt to everlasting remain the Lord of all created things and their Ordainer. Glorified art Thou, O my God! If Thou ceasest to be merciful unto Thy servants, who, then, will show mercy unto them; and if Thou refusest to succor Thy loved ones, who is there that can succor them?

Glorified, immeasurably glorified art Thou! Thou art adored in Thy truth, and Thee do we all, verily, worship; and Thou art manifest in Thy justice, and to Thee do we all, verily, bear witness. Thou art, in truth, beloved in Thy grace. No God is there but Thee, the Help in Peril, the Self-Subsisting.   —*Bahá'u'lláh*

He is God, exalted is He, the Lord of loving-kindness and bounty!

Glory be unto Thee, Thou, O my God, the Lord Omnipotent. I testify to Thine omnipotence and Thy might, Thy sovereignty and Thy loving-kindness, Thy grace and Thy power, the oneness of Thy Being and the unity of Thine Essence, Thy sanctity and exaltation above the world of being and all that is therein.

O my God! Thou seest me detached from all save Thee, holding fast unto Thee and turning unto the ocean of Thy bounty, to the heaven of Thy favor, to the Daystar of Thy grace.

Lord! I bear witness that in Thy servant Thou

hast reposed Thy Trust, and that is the Spirit wherewith Thou hast given life to the world.

I ask of Thee, by the splendor of the Orb of Thy Revelation, mercifully to accept from him that which he hath achieved in Thy days. Grant then that he may be invested with the glory of Thy good-pleasure and adorned with Thine acceptance.

O my Lord! I myself and all created things bear witness unto Thy might, and I pray Thee not to turn away from Thyself this spirit that hath ascended unto Thee, unto Thy heavenly place, Thine exalted Paradise and Thy retreats of nearness, O Thou Who art the Lord of all men!

Grant, then, O my God, that Thy servant may consort with Thy chosen ones, Thy saints and Thy Messengers in heavenly places that the pen cannot tell nor the tongue recount.

O my Lord, the poor one hath verily hastened unto the Kingdom of Thy wealth, the stranger unto his home within Thy precincts, he that is sore athirst to the heavenly river of Thy bounty. Deprive him not, O Lord, from his share of the banquet of Thy grace and from the favor of Thy bounty. Thou art in truth the Almighty, the Gracious, the All-Bountiful.

O my God, Thy Trust hath been returned unto Thee. It behooveth Thy grace and Thy bounty that have compassed Thy dominions on earth and in heaven, to vouchsafe unto Thy newly welcomed one Thy gifts and Thy bestowals, and the fruits of the tree of Thy grace! Powerful art Thou to do as Thou willest, there is none other God but Thee, the Gracious, the Most Bountiful, the Compassionate, the Bestower, the Pardoner, the Precious, the All-Knowing.

I testify, O my Lord, that Thou hast enjoined upon men to honor their guest, and he that hath ascended unto Thee hath verily reached Thee and attained Thy Presence. Deal with him then according to Thy grace and bounty! By Thy glory, I know of a certainty that Thou wilt not withhold Thyself from that which Thou hast commanded Thy servants, nor wilt Thou deprive him that hath clung to the cord of Thy bounty and hath ascended to the Dayspring of Thy wealth.

There is none other God but Thee, the One,

the Single, the Powerful, the Omniscient, the
Bountiful. —*Bahá'u'lláh*

O my God! O Thou forgiver of sins, bestower of gifts, dispeller of afflictions!
Verily, I beseech Thee to forgive the sins of
such as have abandoned the physical garment
and have ascended to the spiritual world.

O my Lord! Purify them from trespasses,
dispel their sorrows, and change their darkness
into light. Cause them to enter the garden of
happiness, cleanse them with the most pure
water, and grant them to behold Thy splendors on the loftiest mount. —*'Abdu'l-Bahá*

O my God! O my God! Verily, Thy servant, humble before the majesty of Thy
divine supremacy, lowly at the door of Thy
oneness, hath believed in Thee and in Thy
verses, hath testified to Thy word, hath been
enkindled with the fire of Thy love, hath
been immersed in the depths of the ocean of
Thy knowledge, hath been attracted by Thy
breezes, hath relied upon Thee, hath turned
his face to Thee, hath offered his supplica-

tions to Thee, and hath been assured of Thy pardon and forgiveness. He hath abandoned this mortal life and hath flown to the kingdom of immortality, yearning for the favor of meeting Thee.

O Lord, glorify his station, shelter him under the pavilion of Thy supreme mercy, cause him to enter Thy glorious paradise, and perpetuate his existence in Thine exalted rose garden, that he may plunge into the sea of light in the world of mysteries.

Verily, Thou art the Generous, the Powerful, the Forgiver and the Bestower.

—'Abdu'l-Bahá

O Thou forgiving Lord! Although some souls have spent the days of their lives in ignorance, and became estranged and contumacious, yet, with one wave from the ocean of Thy forgiveness, all those encompassed by sin will be set free. Whomsoever Thou willest Thou makest a confidant, and whosoever is not the object of Thy choice is accounted a transgressor. Shouldst Thou deal with us with Thy justice, we are all naught but sinners and deserving to be shut out from Thee, but shouldst Thou uphold mercy, every sinner would be made pure and every stranger a friend. Bestow, then, Thy forgiveness and pardon, and grant Thy mercy unto all.

Thou art the Forgiver, the Lightgiver and the Omnipotent. —'Abdu'l-Bahá

FOR WOMEN

O my God, O Forgiver of sins and Dispeller of afflictions! O Thou Who art the Pardoner, the Merciful! I raise my suppliant hands to Thee, tearfully beseeching the court of Thy divine Essence to forgive, through Thy grace and clemency, Thy handmaiden who hath ascended unto the seat of truth. Cause her, O Lord, to be overshadowed by the clouds of Thy bounty and favor, immerse her in the ocean of Thy forgiveness and pardon, and enable her to enter that sanctified abode, Thy heavenly Paradise.

Thou art, verily, the Mighty, the Compassionate, the Generous, the Merciful.

—'Abdu'l-Bahá

O Lord, O Thou Whose mercy hath encompassed all, Whose forgiveness is transcendent, Whose bounty is sublime, Whose pardon and generosity are all-embracing, and the lights of Whose forgiveness are diffused throughout the world! O Lord of glory! I entreat Thee, fervently and tearfully, to cast upon Thy handmaiden who hath ascended unto Thee the glances of the eye of Thy mercy. Robe her in the mantle of Thy grace, bright with the ornaments of the celestial Paradise, and, sheltering her beneath the tree of Thy oneness, illumine her face with the lights of Thy mercy and compassion.

Bestow upon Thy heavenly handmaiden, O God, the holy fragrances born of the spirit of Thy forgiveness. Cause her to dwell in a blissful abode, heal her griefs with the balm of Thy reunion, and, in accordance with Thy will, grant her admission to Thy holy Paradise. Let the angels of Thy loving-kindness descend successively upon her, and shelter her beneath Thy blessed Tree. Thou art, verily, the Ever-Forgiving, the Most Generous, the All-Bountiful.

—'Abdu'l-Bahá

O Thou Kind Lord! This dearly cherished maidservant was attracted to Thee, and through reflection and discernment longed to attain Thy presence and enter Thy realms. With tearful eyes she fixed her gaze on the Kingdom of Mysteries. Many a night she spent in deep communion with Thee, and many a day she lived in intimate remembrance of Thee. At every morn she was mindful of Thee, and at every eve she centered her thoughts upon Thee. Like unto a singing nightingale she chanted Thy sacred verses, and like unto a mirror she sought to reflect Thy light.

O Thou Forgiver of sins! Open Thou the way for this awakened soul to enter Thy Kingdom, and enable this bird, trained by Thy hand, to soar in the eternal rose garden. She is afire with longing to draw nigh unto Thee; enable her to attain Thy presence. She is distraught and distressed in separation from Thee; cause her to be admitted into Thy Heavenly Mansion.

O Lord! We are sinners, but Thou art the Forgiver. We are submerged in the ocean of shortcomings, but Thou art the Pardoner, the Kind. Forgive our sins and bless us with Thine abundant grace. Grant us the privilege of beholding Thy Countenance, and give us the chalice of joy and bliss. We are captives of our own transgressions, and Thou art the King of bountiful favors. We are drowned in a sea of iniquities, and Thou art the Lord of infinite mercy. Thou art the Giver, the Glorious, the Eternal, the Bounteous; and Thou art the All-Gracious, the All-Merciful, the Omnipotent, He Who is the Bestower of gifts and the Forgiver of sins. Verily, Thou art He to Whom we turn for the remission of our failings, He Who is the Lord of lords.   —'Abdu'l-Bahá

DETACHMENT

Suffer me, O my God, to draw nigh unto Thee, and to abide within the precincts of Thy court, for remoteness from Thee hath well-nigh consumed me. Cause me to rest under the shadow of the wings of Thy grace, for the flame of my separation from Thee hath melted my heart within me. Draw me nearer unto the river that is life indeed, for my soul burneth with thirst in its ceaseless search after Thee. My sighs, O my God, proclaim the bitterness of mine anguish, and the tears I shed attest my love for Thee.

I beseech Thee, by the praise wherewith Thou praisest Thyself and the glory wherewith Thou glorifiest Thine own Essence, to grant that we may be numbered among them that have recognized Thee and acknowledged Thy sovereignty in Thy days. Help us then to quaff, O my God, from the fingers of mercy the living waters of Thy loving-kindness, that we may utterly forget all else except Thee, and be occupied only with Thy Self. Powerful art Thou to do what Thou willest. No God is there beside Thee, the Mighty, the Help in Peril, the Self-Subsisting.

Glorified be Thy name, O Thou Who art the King of all Kings! —*Bahá'u'lláh*

Glorified art Thou, O my God! I yield Thee thanks that Thou hast made known unto me Him Who is the Dayspring of Thy mercy, and the Dawning-Place of Thy grace, and the Repository of Thy Cause. I beseech Thee by Thy Name, through which the faces of them that are nigh unto Thee have turned white, and the hearts of such as are devoted to Thee have winged their flight towards Thee, to grant that I may, at all times and under all conditions, lay hold on Thy cord, and be rid of all attachment to anyone except Thee, and may keep mine eyes directed towards the horizon of Thy Revelation, and may carry out what Thou hast prescribed unto me in Thy Tablets.

Attire, O my Lord, both my inner and outer being with the raiment of Thy favors and Thy loving-kindness. Keep me safe, then, from whatsoever may be abhorrent unto Thee, and graciously assist me and my kindred to obey Thee, and to shun whatsoever may stir up any evil or corrupt desire within me.

Thou, truly, art the Lord of all mankind, and the Possessor of this world and of the next. No God is there save Thee, the All-Knowing, the All-Wise.   —*Bahá'u'lláh*

Lauded be Thy name, O my God! I entreat Thee by the fragrances of the Raiment of Thy grace which at Thy bidding and in conformity with Thy desire were diffused throughout the entire creation, and by the Daystar of Thy will that hath shone brightly, through the power of Thy might and of Thy sovereignty, above the horizon of Thy mercy, to blot out from my heart all idle fancies and vain imaginings, that with all my affections I may turn unto Thee, O Thou Lord of all mankind!

I am Thy servant and the son of Thy servant, O my God! I have laid hold on the handle of Thy grace, and clung to the cord of Thy tender mercy. Ordain for me the good things that are with Thee, and nourish me from the Table Thou didst send down out of the clouds of Thy bounty and the heaven of Thy favor.

Thou, in very truth, art the Lord of the worlds, and the God of all that are in heaven and all that are on earth.   —*Bahá'u'lláh*

Many a chilled heart, O my God, hath been set ablaze with the fire of Thy Cause, and many a slumberer hath been wakened by the sweetness of Thy voice. How many are the strangers who have sought shelter beneath the shadow of the tree of Thy oneness, and how numerous the thirsty ones who have panted after the fountain of Thy living waters in Thy days!

Blessed is he that hath set himself towards Thee, and hasted to attain the Dayspring of the lights of Thy face. Blessed is he who with all his affections hath turned to the Dawning-

Place of Thy Revelation and the Fountainhead of Thine inspiration. Blessed is he that hath expended in Thy path what Thou didst bestow upon him through Thy bounty and favor. Blessed is he who, in his sore longing after Thee, hath cast away all else except Thyself. Blessed is he who hath enjoyed intimate communion with Thee, and rid himself of all attachment to anyone save Thee.

I beseech Thee, O my Lord, by Him Who is Thy Name, Who, through the power of Thy sovereignty and might, hath risen above the horizon of His prison, to ordain for everyone what becometh Thee and beseemeth Thine exaltation.

Thy might, in truth, is equal to all things.

— *Bahá'u'lláh*

I know not, O my God, what the Fire is which Thou didst kindle in Thy land. Earth can never cloud its splendor, nor water quench its flame. All the peoples of the world are powerless to resist its force. Great is the blessedness of him that hath drawn nigh unto it, and heard its roaring.

Some, O my God, Thou didst, through Thy strengthening grace, enable to approach it, while others Thou didst keep back by reason of what their hands have wrought in Thy days. Whoso hath hasted towards it and attained unto it hath, in his eagerness to gaze on Thy beauty, yielded his life in Thy path, and ascended unto Thee, wholly detached from aught else except Thyself.

I beseech Thee, O my Lord, by this Fire which blazeth and rageth in the world of creation, to rend asunder the veils that have hindered me from appearing before the throne of Thy majesty, and from standing at the door of Thy gate. Do Thou ordain for me, O my Lord, every good thing Thou didst send down in Thy Book, and suffer me not to be far removed from the shelter of Thy mercy.

Powerful art Thou to do what pleaseth Thee. Thou art, verily, the All-Powerful, the Most Generous.   —*Baháʼuʼlláh*

Praise be unto Thee, O my God! I am one of Thy servants, who hath believed on Thee and on Thy signs. Thou seest how I have set myself towards the door of Thy mercy, and turned my face in the direction of Thy loving-kindness. I beseech Thee, by Thy most excellent titles and Thy most exalted attributes, to open to my face the portals of Thy bestowals. Aid me, then, to do that which is good, O Thou Who art the Possessor of all names and attributes!

I am poor, O my Lord, and Thou art the Rich. I have set my face towards Thee, and detached myself from all but Thee. Deprive me not, I implore Thee, of the breezes of Thy tender mercy, and withhold not from me what Thou didst ordain for the chosen among Thy servants.

Remove the veil from mine eyes, O my Lord, that I may recognize what Thou hast desired for Thy creatures, and discover, in all the manifestations of Thy handiwork, the revelations of Thine almighty power. Enrapture my soul, O my Lord, with Thy most mighty signs, and draw me out of the depths of my corrupt and evil desires. Write down, then, for me the good of this world and of the world to come. Potent art Thou to do what pleaseth Thee. No

God is there but Thee, the All-Glorious, Whose
help is sought by all men.

I yield Thee thanks, O my Lord, that Thou
hast wakened me from my sleep, and stirred
me up, and created in me the desire to perceive
what most of Thy servants have failed to ap-
prehend. Make me able, therefore, O my Lord,
to behold, for love of Thee and for the sake of
Thy pleasure, whatsoever Thou hast desired.
Thou art He to the power of Whose might and
sovereignty all things testify.

There is none other God but Thee, the Almighty, the Beneficent.   *— Bahá'u'lláh*

In the Name of thy Lord, the Creator, the
Sovereign, the All-Sufficing, the Most Exalted, He Whose help is implored by all men.

Say: O my God! O Thou Who art the Maker
of the heavens and of the earth, O Lord of the
Kingdom! Thou well knowest the secrets of my
heart, while Thy Being is inscrutable to all save
Thyself. Thou seest whatsoever is of me, while
no one else can do this save Thee. Vouchsafe
unto me, through Thy grace, what will enable
me to dispense with all except Thee, and des-

tine for me that which will make me independent of everyone else besides Thee. Grant that I may reap the benefit of my life in this world and in the next. Open to my face the portals of Thy grace, and graciously confer upon me Thy tender mercy and bestowals.

O Thou Who art the Lord of grace abounding! Let Thy celestial aid surround those who love Thee, and bestow upon us the gifts and the bounties Thou dost possess. Be Thou sufficient unto us of all things, forgive our sins and have mercy upon us. Thou art our Lord and the Lord of all created things. No one else do we invoke but Thee, and naught do we beseech but Thy favors. Thou art the Lord of bounty and grace, invincible in Thy power and the most skillful in Thy designs. No God is there but Thee, the All-Possessing, the Most Exalted.

Confer Thy blessings, O my Lord, upon the Messengers, the holy ones and the righteous. Verily, Thou art God, the Peerless, the All-Compelling.   — *The Báb*

O Lord! Unto Thee I repair for refuge, and toward all Thy signs I set my heart.

O Lord! Whether traveling or at home, and in my occupation or in my work, I place my whole trust in Thee.

Grant me then Thy sufficing help so as to make me independent of all things, O Thou Who art unsurpassed in Thy mercy!

Bestow upon me my portion, O Lord, as Thou pleasest, and cause me to be satisfied with whatsoever Thou hast ordained for me.

Thine is the absolute authority to command.

— *The Báb*

Say: God sufficeth all things above all things, and nothing in the heavens or in the earth but God sufficeth. Verily, He is in Himself the Knower, the Sustainer, the Omnipotent.

— *The Báb*

O God, my God! Thou art my Hope and my Beloved, my highest Aim and Desire! With great humbleness and entire devotion I pray to Thee to make me a minaret of Thy love in Thy land, a lamp of Thy knowledge among Thy creatures, and a banner of divine bounty in Thy dominion.

Number me with such of Thy servants as have detached themselves from everything but Thee, have sanctified themselves from the transitory things of this world, and have freed themselves from the promptings of the voicers of idle fancies.

Let my heart be dilated with joy through the spirit of confirmation from Thy kingdom, and brighten my eyes by beholding the hosts of divine assistance descending successively upon me from the kingdom of Thine omnipotent glory.

Thou art, in truth, the Almighty, the All-Glorious, the All-Powerful.   — 'Abdu'l-Bahá

O God, my God! Fill up for me the cup of detachment from all things, and in the assembly of Thy splendors and bestowals, rejoice me with the wine of loving Thee. Free me from the assaults of passion and desire, break off from me the shackles of this nether world, draw me with rapture unto Thy supernal realm, and refresh me amongst the handmaids with the breathings of Thy holiness.

O Lord, brighten Thou my face with the lights of Thy bestowals, light Thou mine eyes with beholding the signs of Thine all-subduing might; delight my heart with the glory of Thy knowledge that encompasseth all things, gladden Thou my soul with Thy soul-reviving tidings of great joy, O Thou King of this world and the Kingdom above, O Thou Lord of dominion and might, that I may spread abroad Thy signs and tokens, and proclaim Thy Cause, and promote Thy Teachings, and serve Thy Law and exalt Thy Word.

Thou art, verily, the Powerful, the Ever-Giving, the Able, the Omnipotent.

— *'Abdu'l-Bahá*

EVENING

O my God, my Master, the Goal of my desire! This, Thy servant, seeketh to sleep in the shelter of Thy mercy, and to repose beneath the canopy of Thy grace, imploring Thy care and Thy protection.

I beg of Thee, O my Lord, by Thine eye that sleepeth not, to guard mine eyes from beholding aught beside Thee. Strengthen, then, their vision that they may discern Thy signs, and behold the Horizon of Thy Revelation. Thou art He before the revelations of Whose omnipotence the quintessence of power hath trembled.

No God is there but Thee, the Almighty, the All-Subduing, the Unconditioned.

—*Bahá'u'lláh*

How can I choose to sleep, O God, my God, when the eyes of them that long for Thee are wakeful because of their separation from Thee; and how can I lie down to rest whilst the souls of Thy lovers are sore vexed in their remoteness from Thy presence?

I have committed, O my Lord, my spirit and my entire being into the right hand of Thy might and Thy protection, and I lay my head on my pillow through Thy power, and lift it up according to Thy will and Thy good pleasure. Thou art, in truth, the Preserver, the Keeper, the Almighty, the Most Powerful.

By Thy might! I ask not, whether sleeping or waking, but that which Thou dost desire. I am Thy servant and in Thy hands. Do Thou graciously aid me to do what will shed forth the fragrance of Thy good pleasure. This, truly, is my hope and the hope of them that enjoy near access to Thee. Praised be Thou, O Lord of the worlds!

—*Bahá'u'lláh*

MIDNIGHT

O seeker of Truth! If thou desirest that God may open thine eye, thou must supplicate unto God, pray to and commune with Him at midnight, saying:

O Lord, I have turned my face unto Thy kingdom of oneness and am immersed in the sea of Thy mercy. O Lord, enlighten my sight by beholding Thy lights in this dark night, and make me happy by the wine of Thy love in this wonderful age. O Lord, make me hear Thy call, and open before my face the doors of Thy heaven, so that I may see the light of Thy glory and become attracted to Thy beauty.

Verily, Thou art the Giver, the Generous, the Merciful, the Forgiving. —*'Abdu'l-Bahá*

FAMILIES

Glory be unto Thee, O Lord my God! I beg Thee to forgive me and those who support Thy Faith. Verily, Thou art the sovereign Lord, the Forgiver, the Most Generous. O my God! Enable such servants of Thine as are deprived of knowledge to be admitted into Thy Cause; for once they learn of Thee, they bear witness to the truth of the Day of Judgment and do not dispute the revelations of Thy bounty. Send down upon them the tokens of Thy grace, and grant them, wherever they reside, a liberal share of that which Thou hast ordained for the pious among Thy servants. Thou art in truth the Supreme Ruler, the All-Bounteous, the Most Benevolent.

O my God! Let the outpourings of Thy bounty and blessings descend upon homes whose inmates have embraced Thy Faith, as a token of Thy grace and as a mark of loving-kindness from Thy presence. Verily, unsurpassed art Thou in granting forgiveness. Should Thy bounty be withheld from anyone, how could he be reckoned among the followers of the Faith in Thy Day?

Bless me, O my God, and those who will believe in Thy signs on the appointed Day, and such as cherish my love in their hearts—a love which Thou dost instill into them. Verily, Thou art the Lord of righteousness, the Most Exalted.

— *The Báb*

PARENTS

I beg Thy forgiveness, O my God, and implore pardon after the manner Thou wishest Thy servants to direct themselves to Thee. I beg of Thee to wash away our sins as befitteth Thy Lordship, and to forgive me, my parents, and those who in Thy estimation have entered the abode of Thy love in a manner which is worthy of Thy transcendent sovereignty and well beseemeth the glory of Thy celestial power.

O my God! Thou hast inspired my soul to offer its supplication to Thee, and but for Thee, I would not call upon Thee. Lauded and glorified art Thou; I yield Thee praise inasmuch as Thou didst reveal Thyself unto me, and I beg Thee to forgive me, since I have fallen short in my duty to know Thee and have failed to walk in the path of Thy love. — *The Báb*

O Lord! In this Most Great Dispensation Thou dost accept the intercession of children in behalf of their parents. This is one of the special infinite bestowals of this Dispensation. Therefore, O Thou kind Lord, accept the request of this Thy servant at the threshold of Thy singleness and submerge his father in the ocean of Thy grace, because this son hath arisen to render Thee service and is exerting effort at all times in the pathway of Thy love. Verily, Thou art the Giver, the Forgiver and the Kind! — *'Abdu'l-Bahá*

HUSBANDS

O God, my God! This Thy handmaid is calling upon Thee, trusting in Thee, turning her face unto Thee, imploring Thee to shed Thy heavenly bounties upon her, and to disclose unto her Thy spiritual mysteries, and to cast upon her the lights of Thy Godhead.

O my Lord! Make the eyes of my husband to see. Rejoice Thou his heart with the light of the knowledge of Thee, draw Thou his mind unto Thy luminous beauty, cheer Thou his spirit by revealing unto him Thy manifest splendors.

O my Lord! Lift Thou the veil from before his sight. Rain down Thy plenteous bounties upon him, intoxicate him with the wine of love for Thee, make him one of Thy angels whose feet walk upon this earth even as their souls are soaring through the high heavens. Cause him to become a brilliant lamp, shining out with the light of Thy wisdom in the midst of Thy people.

Verily, Thou art the Precious, the Ever-Bestowing, the Open of Hand.   —'Abdu'l-Bahá

FIRMNESS IN THE COVENANT

Glory be to Thee, O King of eternity, and the Maker of nations, and the Fashioner of every moldering bone! I pray Thee, by Thy Name through which Thou didst call all mankind unto the horizon of Thy majesty and glory, and didst guide Thy servants to the court of Thy grace and favors, to number me with such as have rid themselves from everything except Thyself, and have set themselves towards Thee, and have not been kept back by such misfortunes as were decreed by Thee, from turning in the direction of Thy gifts.

I have laid hold, O my Lord, on the handle of Thy bounty, and clung steadfastly to the hem of the robe of Thy favor. Send down, then, upon me, out of the clouds of Thy generosity, what will purge out from me the remembrance of anyone except Thee, and make me able to turn unto Him Who is the Object of the adoration of all mankind, against Whom have been arrayed the stirrers of sedition, who have broken Thy covenant, and disbelieved in Thee and in Thy signs.

Deny me not, O my Lord, the fragrances of Thy raiment in Thy days, and deprive me not of the breathings of Thy Revelation at the appearance of the splendors of the light of Thy face. Powerful art Thou to do what pleaseth Thee. Naught can resist Thy will, nor frustrate what Thou hast purposed by Thy power.

No God is there but Thee, the Almighty, the All-Wise.   —*Bahá'u'lláh*

He is the Mighty, the Pardoner, the Compassionate!

O God, my God! Thou beholdest Thy servants in the abyss of perdition and error; where is Thy light of divine guidance, O Thou the Desire of the world? Thou knowest their helplessness and their feebleness; where is Thy power, O Thou in Whose grasp lie the powers of heaven and earth?

I ask Thee, O Lord my God, by the splendor of the lights of Thy loving-kindness and the billows of the ocean of Thy knowledge and wisdom and by Thy Word wherewith Thou hast swayed the peoples of Thy dominion, to grant that I may be one of them that have observed Thy bidding in Thy Book. And do Thou ordain for me that which Thou hast ordained for Thy trusted ones, them that have quaffed the wine of divine inspiration from the chalice of Thy bounty and hastened to do Thy pleasure and observe Thy Covenant and Testament. Powerful art Thou to do as Thou willest. There is none other God but Thee, the All-Knowing, the All-Wise.

Decree for me, by Thy bounty, O Lord, that which shall prosper me in this world and hereafter and shall draw me nigh unto Thee, O Thou Who art the Lord of all men. There is none other God but Thee, the One, the Mighty, the Glorified.   *— Bahá'u'lláh*

Make firm our steps, O Lord, in Thy path and strengthen Thou our hearts in Thine obedience. Turn our faces toward the beauty of Thy oneness, and gladden our bosoms with the signs of Thy divine unity. Adorn our bodies with the robe of Thy bounty, and remove from our eyes the veil of sinfulness, and give us the chalice of Thy grace; that the essence of all beings may sing Thy praise before the vision of Thy grandeur. Reveal then Thyself, O Lord, by Thy merciful utterance and the mystery of Thy divine being, that the holy ecstasy of prayer may fill our souls—a prayer that shall rise above words and letters and transcend the murmur of syllables and sounds—that all things may be merged into nothingness before the revelation of Thy splendor.

Lord! These are servants that have remained fast and firm in Thy Covenant and Thy Testament, that have held fast unto the cord of constancy in Thy Cause and clung unto the hem of the robe of Thy grandeur. Assist them, O Lord, with Thy grace, confirm them with Thy power and strengthen their loins in obedience to Thee.

Thou art the Pardoner, the Gracious.

—*'Abdu'l-Bahá*

O compassionate God! Thanks be to Thee for Thou hast awakened and made me conscious. Thou hast given me a seeing eye and favored me with a hearing ear, hast led me to Thy kingdom and guided me to Thy path. Thou hast shown me the right way and caused me to enter the ark of deliverance. O God! Keep me steadfast and make me firm and staunch. Protect me from violent tests and preserve and shelter me in the strongly fortified fortress of Thy Covenant and Testament. Thou art the Powerful. Thou art the Seeing. Thou art the Hearing.

O Thou the Compassionate God. Bestow upon me a heart which, like unto a glass, may be illumined with the light of Thy love, and confer upon me thoughts which may change this world into a rose garden through the outpourings of heavenly grace.

Thou art the Compassionate, the Merciful. Thou art the Great Beneficent God.

— 'Abdu'l-Bahá

O my Lord and my Hope! Help Thou Thy loved ones to be steadfast in Thy

mighty Covenant, to remain faithful to Thy
manifest Cause, and to carry out the commandments Thou didst set down for them in
Thy Book of Splendors; that they may become banners of guidance and lamps of the
Company above, wellsprings of Thine infinite wisdom, and stars that lead aright, as
they shine down from the supernal sky.

Verily, art Thou the Invincible, the Almighty, the All-Powerful.   — 'Abdu'l-Bahá

FORGIVENESS

Glorified art Thou, O Lord my God! I beseech Thee by Thy Chosen Ones, and by the Bearers of Thy Trust, and by Him Whom Thou hast ordained to be the Seal of Thy Prophets and of Thy Messengers, to let Thy remembrance be my companion, and Thy love my aim, and Thy face my goal, and Thy name my lamp, and Thy wish my desire, and Thy pleasure my delight.

I am a sinner, O my Lord, and Thou art the Ever-Forgiving. As soon as I recognized Thee, I hastened to attain the exalted court of Thy loving-kindness. Forgive me, O my Lord, my sins which have hindered me from walking in the ways of Thy good pleasure, and from attaining the shores of the ocean of Thy oneness.

There is no one, O my Lord, who can deal bountifully with me to whom I can turn my face, and none who can have compassion on me that I may crave his mercy. Cast me not out, I implore Thee, of the presence of Thy grace, neither do Thou withhold from me the outpourings of Thy generosity and bounty. Ordain for me, O my Lord, what Thou hast ordained for them that love Thee, and write down for me what Thou hast written down for Thy chosen ones. My gaze hath, at all times, been fixed on the horizon of Thy gracious providence, and mine eyes bent upon the court of Thy tender mercies. Do with me as beseemeth Thee. No God is there but Thee, the God of power, the God of glory, Whose help is implored by all men.   —*Bahá'u'lláh*

I am he, O my Lord, that hath set his face towards Thee, and fixed his hope on the wonders of Thy grace and the revelations of Thy bounty. I pray Thee that Thou wilt not suffer me to turn away disappointed from the door of Thy mercy, nor abandon me to such of Thy creatures as have repudiated Thy Cause.

I am, O my God, Thy servant and the son

of Thy servant. I have recognized Thy truth in Thy days, and have directed my steps towards the shores of Thy oneness, confessing Thy singleness, acknowledging Thy unity, and hoping for Thy forgiveness and pardon. Powerful art Thou to do what Thou willest; no God is there beside Thee, the All-Glorious, the Ever-Forgiving.   —*Bahá'u'lláh*

Thou seest me, O my Lord, with my face turned towards the heaven of Thy bounty and the ocean of Thy favor, withdrawn from all else beside Thee. I ask of Thee, by the splendors of the Sun of Thy revelation on Sinai, and the effulgences of the Orb of Thy grace which shineth from the horizon of Thy Name, the Ever-Forgiving, to grant me Thy pardon and to have mercy upon me. Write down, then, for me with Thy pen of glory that which will exalt me through Thy Name in the world of creation. Aid me, O my Lord, to set myself towards Thee, and to hearken unto the voice of Thy loved ones, whom the powers of the earth have failed to weaken, and the dominion of the nations has been powerless to withhold from Thee, and who, advancing towards Thee, have said: "God is our Lord, the Lord of all who are in heaven and all who are on earth."

—*Bahá'u'lláh*

Glorified art Thou, O Lord my God! Every time I venture to make mention of Thee, I am held back by my mighty sins and grievous trespasses against Thee, and find myself wholly deprived of Thy grace, and utterly powerless to celebrate Thy praise. My great confidence in Thy bounty, however, reviveth my hope in Thee, and my certitude that Thou wilt bountifully deal with me emboldeneth me to extol Thee, and to ask of Thee the things Thou dost possess.

I implore Thee, O my God, by Thy mercy that hath surpassed all created things, and to which all that are immersed beneath the oceans of Thy names bear witness, not to abandon me unto my self, for my heart is prone to evil. Guard me, then, within the stronghold of Thy protection and the shelter of Thy care. I am he, O my God, whose only wish is what Thou hast determined by the power of Thy might. All I have chosen for myself is to be assisted by Thy gracious appointments and the ruling of Thy will, and to be aided with the tokens of Thy decree and judgment.

I beseech Thee, O Thou Who art the Beloved of the hearts which long for Thee, by the Manifestations of Thy Cause and the Day-springs of Thine inspiration, and the Exponents of Thy majesty, and the Treasuries of Thy knowledge, not to suffer me to be deprived of Thy holy Habitation, Thy Fane and Thy Tabernacle. Aid me, O my Lord, to attain His hallowed court, and to circle round His person, and to stand humbly at His door.

Thou art He Whose power is from everlasting to everlasting. Nothing escapeth Thy knowledge. Thou art, verily, the God of power, the God of glory and wisdom.

Praised be God, the Lord of the worlds!

—*Bahá'u'lláh*

Lauded be Thy name, O my God and the God of all things, my Glory and the Glory of all things, my Desire and the Desire of all things, my Strength and the Strength of all things, my King and the King of all things, my Possessor and the Possessor of all things, my Aim and the Aim of all things, my Mover and the Mover of all things! Suffer me not, I implore Thee, to be kept back from the ocean of Thy tender mercies, nor to be far removed from the shores of nearness to Thee.

Aught else except Thee, O my Lord, profiteth me not, and near access to anyone save Thyself availeth me nothing. I entreat Thee by the plenteousness of Thy riches, whereby Thou didst dispense with all else except Thyself, to number me with such as have set their faces towards Thee, and arisen to serve Thee.

Forgive, then, O my Lord, Thy servants and Thy handmaidens. Thou, truly, art the Ever-Forgiving, the Most Compassionate.

—*Bahá'u'lláh*

O God our Lord! Protect us through Thy grace from whatsoever may be repugnant unto Thee, and vouchsafe unto us that which well beseemeth Thee. Give us more out of Thy bounty, and bless us. Pardon us for the things we have done, and wash away our sins, and forgive us with Thy gracious forgiveness. Verily, Thou art the Most Exalted, the Self-Subsisting.

Thy loving providence hath encompassed all created things in the heavens and on the earth, and Thy forgiveness hath surpassed the whole creation. Thine is sovereignty; in Thy hand are the Kingdoms of Creation and Revelation; in Thy right hand Thou holdest all created things, and within Thy grasp are the assigned measures of forgiveness. Thou forgivest whomsoever among Thy servants Thou pleasest. Verily, Thou art the Ever-Forgiving, the All-Loving. Nothing whatsoever escapeth Thy knowledge, and naught is there which is hidden from Thee.

O God our Lord! Protect us through the potency of Thy might, enable us to enter Thy wondrous surging ocean, and grant us that which well befitteth Thee.

Thou art the Sovereign Ruler, the Mighty Doer, the Exalted, the All-Loving.

— *The Báb*

Praise be unto Thee, O Lord. Forgive us our sins, have mercy upon us and enable us to return unto Thee. Suffer us not to rely on aught else besides Thee, and vouchsafe unto us, through Thy bounty, that which Thou lovest and desirest and well beseemeth Thee. Exalt the station of them that have truly believed, and forgive them with Thy gracious forgiveness. Verily, Thou art the Help in Peril, the Self-Subsisting.

— The Báb

I beg Thee to forgive me, O my Lord, for every mention but the mention of Thee, and for every praise but the praise of Thee, and for every delight but delight in Thy nearness, and for every pleasure but the pleasure of communion with Thee, and for every joy but the joy of Thy love and of Thy good-pleasure, and for all things pertaining unto me which bear no relationship unto Thee, O Thou Who art the Lord of lords, He Who provideth the means and unlocketh the doors.

— The Báb

Glory be unto Thee, O God. How can I make mention of Thee while Thou art sanctified from the praise of all mankind. Magnified be Thy Name, O God, Thou art the King, the Eternal Truth; Thou knowest what is in the heavens and on the earth, and unto Thee must all return. Thou hast sent down Thy divinely ordained Revelation according to a clear measure. Praised art Thou, O Lord! At Thy behest Thou dost render victorious whomsoever Thou willest, through the hosts of heaven and earth and whatsoever existeth between them. Thou art the Sovereign, the Eternal Truth, the Lord of invincible might.

Glorified art Thou, O Lord! Thou forgivest at all times the sins of such among Thy servants as implore Thy pardon. Wash away my sins and the sins of those who seek Thy forgiveness at dawn, who pray to Thee in the daytime and in the night season, who yearn after naught save God, who offer up whatsoever God hath graciously bestowed upon them, who celebrate Thy praise at morn and eventide, and who are not remiss in their duties.

— *The Báb*

I am aware, O Lord, that my trespasses have covered my face with shame in Thy presence, and have burdened my back before Thee, have intervened between me and Thy beauteous countenance, have compassed me from every direction and have hindered me on all sides from gaining access unto the revelations of Thy celestial power.

O Lord! If Thou forgivest me not, who is there then to grant pardon, and if Thou hast no mercy upon me who is capable of showing compassion? Glory be unto Thee, Thou didst create me when I was non-existent and Thou didst nourish me while I was devoid of any understanding. Praise be unto Thee, every evidence of bounty proceedeth from Thee and every token of grace emanateth from the treasuries of Thy decree.   — *The Báb*

O Thou forgiving Lord! Thou art the shelter of all these Thy servants. Thou knowest the secrets and art aware of all things. We are all helpless, and Thou art the Mighty, the Omnipotent. We are all sinners, and Thou art the Forgiver of sins, the Merciful, the Compassionate. O Lord! Look not at our shortcomings. Deal with us according to Thy grace and bounty. Our shortcomings are many, but the ocean of Thy forgiveness is boundless. Our weakness is grievous, but the evidences of Thine aid and assistance are clear. Therefore, confirm and strengthen us. Enable us to do that which is worthy of Thy holy Threshold. Illumine our hearts, grant us discerning eyes and attentive ears. Resuscitate the dead and heal the sick. Bestow wealth upon the poor and give peace and security to the fearful. Accept us in Thy kingdom and illumine us with the light of guidance. Thou art the Powerful and the Omnipotent. Thou art the Generous. Thou art the Clement. Thou art the Kind.

— 'Abdu'l-Bahá

THE FUND

All the friends of God . . . should contribute to the extent possible, however modest their offering may be. God doth not burden a soul beyond its capacity. Such contributions must come from all centers and all believers. . . . O Friends of God! Be ye assured that in place of these contributions, your agriculture, your industry, and your commerce will be blessed by manifold increases, with goodly gifts and bestowals. He who cometh with one goodly deed will receive a tenfold reward. There is no doubt that the living Lord will abundantly confirm those who expend their wealth in His path.

O God, my God! Illumine the brows of Thy true lovers, and support them with angelic hosts of certain triumph. Set firm their feet on Thy straight path, and out of Thine ancient bounty open before them the portals of Thy blessings; for they are expending on Thy pathway what Thou hast bestowed upon them, safeguarding Thy Faith, putting their trust in their remembrance of Thee, offering up their hearts for love of Thee, and withholding not what they possess in adoration for Thy Beauty and in their search for ways to please Thee.

O my Lord! Ordain for them a plenteous share, a destined recompense and sure reward.

Verily, Thou art the Sustainer, the Helper, the Generous, the Bountiful, the Ever-Bestowing. —'Abdu'l-Bahá

GATHERINGS

Glorified art Thou, O Lord my God! I implore Thee by the onrushing winds of Thy grace, and by them Who are the Day-springs of Thy purpose and the Dawning-Places of Thine inspiration, to send down upon me and upon all that have sought Thy face that which beseemeth Thy generosity and bountiful grace, and is worthy of Thy bestowals and favors. Poor and desolate I am, O my Lord! Immerse me in the ocean of Thy wealth; athirst, suffer me to drink from the living waters of Thy loving-kindness.

I beseech Thee, by Thine own Self and by Him Whom Thou hast appointed as the Mani-festation of Thine own Being and Thy discrimi-nating Word unto all that are in heaven and on earth, to gather together Thy servants beneath the shade of the Tree of Thy gracious provi-dence. Help them, then, to partake of its fruits, to incline their ears to the rustling of its leaves, and to the sweetness of the voice of the Bird that chanteth upon its branches. Thou art, verily, the Help in Peril, the Inaccessible, the Almighty, the Most Bountiful. —*Bahá'u'lláh*

O Thou merciful God! O Thou Who art mighty and powerful! O Thou most kind Father! These servants have gathered together, turning to Thee, supplicating Thy threshold, desiring Thine endless bounties from Thy great assurance. They have no purpose save Thy good pleasure. They have no intention save service to the world of humanity.

O God! Make this assemblage radiant. Make the hearts merciful. Confer the bounties of the Holy Spirit. Endow them with a power from heaven. Bless them with heavenly minds. Increase their sincerity, so that with all humility and contrition they may turn to Thy kingdom and be occupied with service to the world of humanity. May each one become a radiant candle. May each one become a brilliant star. May each one become beautiful in color and redolent of fragrance in the kingdom of God.

O kind Father! Confer Thy blessings. Consider not our shortcomings. Shelter us under Thy protection. Remember not our sins. Heal us with Thy mercy. We are weak; Thou art mighty. We are poor; Thou art rich. We are sick; Thou art the Physician. We are needy; Thou art most generous.

O God! Endow us with Thy providence. Thou art the Powerful. Thou art the Giver. Thou art the Beneficent.   —'Abdu'l-Bahá

O Thou kind Lord! These are Thy servants who have gathered in this meeting, have turned unto Thy kingdom and are in need of Thy bestowal and blessing. O Thou God! Manifest and make evident the signs of Thy oneness which have been deposited in all the realities of life. Reveal and unfold the virtues which Thou hast made latent and concealed in these human realities.

O God! We are as plants, and Thy bounty is as the rain; refresh and cause these plants to grow through Thy bestowal. We are Thy servants; free us from the fetters of material exist-

ence. We are ignorant; make us wise. We are
dead; make us alive. We are material; endow
us with spirit. We are deprived; make us the
intimates of Thy mysteries. We are needy; enrich and bless us from Thy boundless treasury.
O God! Resuscitate us; give us sight; give us
hearing; familiarize us with the mysteries of life,
so that the secrets of Thy kingdom may become revealed to us in this world of existence
and we may confess Thy oneness. Every bestowal emanates from Thee; every benediction
is Thine.

Thou art mighty. Thou art powerful. Thou
art the Giver, and Thou art the Ever-Bounte-
ous.   — 'Abdu'l-Bahá

O my God! O my God! Verily, these servants are turning to Thee, supplicating
Thy kingdom of mercy. Verily, they are attracted by Thy holiness and set aglow with
the fire of Thy love, seeking confirmation
from Thy wondrous kingdom, and hoping
for attainment in Thy heavenly realm. Verily,
they long for the descent of Thy bestowal,
desiring illumination from the Sun of Real-

ity. O Lord! Make them radiant lamps, merciful signs, fruitful trees and shining stars. May they come forth in Thy service and be connected with Thee by the bonds and ties of Thy love, longing for the lights of Thy favor. O Lord! Make them signs of guidance, standards of Thine immortal kingdom, waves of the sea of Thy mercy, mirrors of the light of Thy majesty.

Verily, Thou art the Generous. Verily, Thou art the Merciful. Verily, Thou art the Precious, the Beloved.   —'Abdu'l-Bahá

O Thou forgiving God! These servants are turning to Thy kingdom and seeking Thy grace and bounty. O God! Make their hearts good and pure in order that they may become worthy of Thy love. Purify and sanctify the spirits that the light of the Sun of Reality may shine upon them. Purify and sanctify the eyes that they may perceive Thy light. Purify and sanctify the ears in order that they may hear the call of Thy kingdom.

O Lord! Verily, we are weak, but Thou art mighty. Verily, we are poor, but Thou art rich.

We are the seekers, and Thou art the One sought. O Lord! Have compassion upon us and forgive us; bestow upon us such capacity and receptiveness that we may be worthy of Thy favors and become attracted to Thy kingdom, that we may drink deep of the water of life, may be enkindled by the fire of Thy love, and be resuscitated through the breaths of the Holy Spirit in this radiant century.

O God, my God! Cast upon this gathering the glances of Thy loving-kindness. Keep safe each and all in Thy custody and under Thy protection. Send down upon these souls Thy heavenly blessings. Immerse them in the ocean of Thy mercy, and quicken them through the breaths of the Holy Spirit.

O Lord! Bestow Thy gracious aid and confirmation upon this just government. This country lieth beneath the sheltering shadow of Thy protection, and this people is in Thy service. O Lord! Confer upon them Thy heavenly bounty and render the outpourings of Thy grace and favor copious and abundant. Suffer this esteemed nation to be held in honor, and enable it to be admitted into Thy kingdom.

Thou art the Powerful, the Omnipotent, the Merciful, and Thou art the Generous, the Beneficent, the Lord of grace abounding.

— *'Abdu'l-Bahá*

O Divine Providence! This assemblage is composed of Thy friends who are attracted to Thy beauty and are set ablaze by the fire of Thy love. Turn these souls into heavenly angels, resuscitate them through the breath of Thy Holy Spirit, grant them eloquent tongues and resolute hearts, bestow upon them heavenly power and merciful susceptibilities, cause them to become the promulgators of the oneness of mankind and the cause of love and concord in the world of humanity, so that the perilous darkness of ignorant prejudice may vanish through the light of the Sun of Truth, this dreary world may become illumined, this material realm may absorb the rays of the world of spirit, these different colors may merge into one color and the melody of praise may rise to the kingdom of Thy sanctity.

Verily, Thou art the Omnipotent and the Almighty! —'Abdu'l-Bahá

O Thou loving Provider! These souls have hearkened to the summons of the Kingdom, and have gazed upon the glory of the Sun of Truth. They have risen upward to the refreshing skies of love; they are enamored of Thy nature, and they worship Thy beauty. Unto Thee have they turned themselves, speaking together of Thee, seeking out Thy dwelling, and thirsting for the waterbrooks of Thy heavenly realm.

Thou art the Giver, the Bestower, the Ever-Loving. —'Abdu'l-Bahá

THE NINETEEN DAY FEAST

O God! Dispel all those elements which are the cause of discord, and prepare for us all those things which are the cause of unity and accord! O God! Descend upon us Heavenly Fragrance and change this gathering into a gathering of Heaven! Grant to us

every benefit and every food. Prepare for us the Food of Love! Give us the Food of Knowledge! Bestow on us the Food of Heavenly Illumination!
— *'Abdu'l-Bahá*

HEALING

O God, my God! I beg of Thee by the ocean of Thy healing, and by the splendors of the Daystar of Thy grace, and by Thy Name through which Thou didst subdue Thy servants, and by the pervasive power of Thy most exalted Word and the potency of Thy most august Pen, and by Thy mercy that hath preceded the creation of all who are in heaven and on earth, to purge me with the waters of Thy bounty from every affliction and disorder, and from all weakness and feebleness.

Thou seest, O my Lord, Thy suppliant waiting at the door of Thy bounty, and him who hath set his hopes on Thee clinging to the cord of Thy generosity. Deny him not, I beseech Thee, the things he seeketh from the ocean of Thy grace and the Daystar of Thy loving-kindness.

Powerful art Thou to do what pleaseth Thee.
There is none other God save Thee, the Ever-
Forgiving, the Most Generous.　　—*Bahá'u'lláh*

Thy name is my healing, O my God, and
remembrance of Thee is my remedy.
Nearness to Thee is my hope, and love for
Thee is my companion. Thy mercy to me is
my healing and my succor in both this world
and the world to come. Thou, verily, art the
All-Bountiful, the All-Knowing, the All-Wise.
　　　　　　　　　　　　　　—*Bahá'u'lláh*

Glory be to Thee, O Lord my God! I implore Thee by Thy Name, through
which Thou didst lift up the ensigns of Thy
guidance, and didst shed the radiance of Thy
loving-kindness, and didst reveal the sovereignty of Thy Lordship; through which the
lamp of Thy names hath appeared within the
niche of Thine attributes, and He Who is the
Tabernacle of Thy unity and the Manifestation of detachment hath shone forth;
through which the ways of Thy guidance
were made known, and the paths of Thy

good pleasure were marked out; through
which the foundations of error have been
made to tremble, and the signs of wickedness
have been abolished; through which the
fountains of wisdom have burst forth, and
the heavenly table hath been sent down;
through which Thou didst preserve Thy servants and didst vouchsafe Thy healing;
through which Thou didst show forth Thy
tender mercies unto Thy servants and re-
vealedst Thy forgiveness amidst Thy creatures—I implore Thee to keep safe him who
hath held fast and returned unto Thee, and
clung to Thy mercy, and seized the hem of
Thy loving providence. Send down, then,
upon him Thy healing, and make him
whole, and endue him with a constancy
vouchsafed by Thee, and a tranquillity bestowed by Thy highness.

Thou art, verily, the Healer, the Preserver,
the Helper, the Almighty, the Powerful, the All-
Glorious, the All-Knowing. —*Bahá'u'lláh*

Praised be Thou, O Lord my God! I implore Thee, by Thy Most Great Name

through which Thou didst stir up Thy servants and build up Thy cities, and by Thy most excellent titles, and Thy most august attributes, to assist Thy people to turn in the direction of Thy manifold bounties, and set their faces towards the Tabernacle of Thy wisdom. Heal Thou the sicknesses that have assailed the souls on every side, and have deterred them from directing their gaze towards the Paradise that lieth in the shelter of Thy shadowing Name, which Thou didst ordain to be the King of all names unto all who are in heaven and all who are on earth. Potent art Thou to do as pleaseth Thee. In Thy hands is the empire of all names. There is none other God but Thee, the Mighty, the Wise.

I am but a poor creature, O my Lord; I have clung to the hem of Thy riches. I am sore sick; I have held fast the cord of Thy healing. Deliver me from the ills that have encircled me, and wash me thoroughly with the waters of Thy graciousness and mercy, and attire me with the raiment of wholesomeness, through Thy forgiveness and bounty. Fix, then, mine eyes upon Thee, and rid me of all attachment to aught else except Thyself. Aid me to do what Thou desirest, and to fulfill what Thou pleasest.

Thou art truly the Lord of this life and of the next. Thou art, in truth, the Ever-Forgiving, the Most Merciful. —*Bahá'u'lláh*

FOR WOMEN

Glory be to Thee, O Lord my God! I beg of Thee by Thy Name through which He Who is Thy Beauty hath been stablished upon the throne of Thy Cause, and by Thy Name through which Thou changest all things, and gatherest together all things, and callest to account all things, and rewardest all things, and preservest all things, and sustainest all things—I beg of Thee to guard this handmaiden who hath fled for refuge to Thee, and hath sought the shelter of Him in Whom Thou Thyself art manifest, and hath put her whole trust and confidence in Thee.

She is sick, O my God, and hath entered beneath the shadow of the Tree of Thy healing; afflicted, and hath fled to the City of Thy

protection; diseased, and hath sought the Fountainhead of Thy favors; sorely vexed, and hath
hasted to attain the Wellspring of Thy tranquillity; burdened with sin, and hath set her
face toward the court of Thy forgiveness.

Attire her, by Thy sovereignty and Thy loving-kindness, O my God and my Beloved, with
the raiment of Thy balm and Thy healing, and
make her quaff of the cup of Thy mercy and
Thy favors. Protect her, moreover, from every
affliction and ailment, from all pain and sickness, and from whatsoever may be abhorrent
unto Thee.

Thou, in truth, art immensely exalted above
all else except Thyself. Thou art, verily, the
Healer, the All-Sufficing, the Preserver, the
Ever-Forgiving, the Most Merciful.

—*Bahá'u'lláh*

FOR INFANTS

Thou art He, O my God, through Whose
names the sick are healed and the ailing
are restored, and the thirsty are given drink,

and the sore-vexed are tranquilized, and the wayward are guided, and the abased are exalted, and the poor are enriched, and the ignorant are enlightened, and the gloomy are illumined, and the sorrowful are cheered, and the chilled are warmed, and the downtrodden are raised up. Through Thy name, O my God, all created things were stirred up, and the heavens were spread, and the earth was established, and the clouds were raised and made to rain upon the earth. This, verily, is a token of Thy grace unto all Thy creatures.

I implore Thee, therefore, by Thy name through which Thou didst manifest Thy Godhead, and didst exalt Thy Cause above all creation, and by each of Thy most excellent titles and most august attributes, and by all the virtues wherewith Thy transcendent and most exalted Being is extolled, to send down this night from the clouds of Thy mercy the rains of Thy healing upon this suckling, whom Thou hast related unto Thine all-glorious Self in the kingdom of Thy creation. Clothe him, then, O my God, by Thy grace, with the robe of well-

being and health, and guard him, O my Beloved, from every affliction and disorder, and
from whatsoever is obnoxious unto Thee. Thy
might, verily, is equal to all things. Thou, in
truth, art the Most Powerful, the Self-Subsisting. Send down, moreover, upon him, O my
God, the good of this world and of the next,
and the good of the former and latter generations. Thy might and Thy wisdom are, verily,
equal unto this. — *Bahá'u'lláh*

THE LONG HEALING PRAYER

He is the Healer, the Sufficer, the Helper,
the All-Forgiving, the All-Merciful.

I call on Thee O Exalted One, O Faithful
One, O Glorious One! Thou the Sufficing,
Thou the Healing, Thou the Abiding, O Thou
Abiding One!

I call on Thee O Sovereign, O Upraiser, O
Judge! Thou the Sufficing, Thou the Healing,
Thou the Abiding, O Thou Abiding One!

I call on Thee O Peerless One, O Eternal

One, O Single One! Thou the Sufficing, Thou the Healing, Thou the Abiding, O Thou Abiding One!

I call on Thee O Most Praised One, O Holy One, O Helping One! Thou the Sufficing, Thou the Healing, Thou the Abiding, O Thou Abiding One!

I call on Thee O Omniscient, O Most Wise, O Most Great One! Thou the Sufficing, Thou the Healing, Thou the Abiding, O Thou Abiding One!

I call on Thee O Clement One, O Majestic One, O Ordaining One! Thou the Sufficing, Thou the Healing, Thou the Abiding, O Thou Abiding One!

I call on Thee O Beloved One, O Cherished One, O Enraptured One! Thou the Sufficing, Thou the Healing, Thou the Abiding, O Thou Abiding One!

I call on Thee O Mightiest One, O Sustaining One, O Potent One! Thou the Sufficing, Thou the Healing, Thou the Abiding, O Thou Abiding One!

I call on Thee O Ruling One, O Self-Subsisting, O All-Knowing One! Thou the Sufficing, Thou the Healing, Thou the Abiding, O Thou Abiding One!

I call on Thee O Spirit, O Light, O Most Manifest One! Thou the Sufficing, Thou the Healing, Thou the Abiding, O Thou Abiding One!

I call on Thee O Thou Frequented by all, O Thou Known to all, O Thou Hidden from all! Thou the Sufficing, Thou the Healing, Thou the Abiding, O Thou Abiding One!

I call on Thee O Concealed One, O Triumphant One, O Bestowing One! Thou the Sufficing, Thou the Healing, Thou the Abiding, O Thou Abiding One!

I call on Thee O Almighty, O Succoring One, O Concealing One! Thou the Sufficing, Thou the Healing, Thou the Abiding, O Thou Abiding One!

I call on Thee O Fashioner, O Satisfier, O Uprooter! Thou the Sufficing, Thou the Healing, Thou the Abiding, O Thou Abiding One!

I call on Thee O Rising One, O Gathering One, O Exalting One! Thou the Sufficing, Thou the Healing, Thou the Abiding, O Thou Abiding One!

I call on Thee O Perfecting One, O Unfettered One, O Bountiful One! Thou the Sufficing, Thou the Healing, Thou the Abiding, O Thou Abiding One!

I call on Thee O Beneficent One, O Withholding One, O Creating One! Thou the Sufficing, Thou the Healing, Thou the Abiding, O Thou Abiding One!

I call on Thee O Most Sublime One, O Beauteous One, O Bounteous One! Thou the Sufficing, Thou the Healing, Thou the Abiding, O Thou Abiding One!

I call on Thee O Just One, O Gracious One, O Generous One! Thou the Sufficing, Thou the Healing, Thou the Abiding, O Thou Abiding One!

I call on Thee O All-Compelling, O Ever-Abiding, O Most Knowing One! Thou the Sufficing, Thou the Healing, Thou the Abiding, O Thou Abiding One!

I call on Thee O Magnificent One, O Ancient of Days, O Magnanimous One! Thou the Sufficing, Thou the Healing, Thou the Abiding, O Thou Abiding One!

I call on Thee O Well-Guarded One, O Lord

of Joy, O Desired One! Thou the Sufficing, Thou the Healing, Thou the Abiding, O Thou Abiding One!

I call on Thee O Thou Kind to all, O Thou Compassionate with all, O Most Benevolent One! Thou the Sufficing, Thou the Healing, Thou the Abiding, O Thou Abiding One!

I call on Thee O Haven for all, O Shelter to all, O All-Preserving One! Thou the Sufficing, Thou the Healing, Thou the Abiding, O Thou Abiding One!

I call on Thee O Thou Succorer of all, O Thou Invoked by all, O Quickening One! Thou the Sufficing, Thou the Healing, Thou the Abiding, O Thou Abiding One!

I call on Thee O Unfolder, O Ravager, O Most Clement One! Thou the Sufficing, Thou the Healing, Thou the Abiding, O Thou Abiding One!

I call on Thee O Thou my Soul, O Thou my Beloved, O Thou my Faith! Thou the Sufficing, Thou the Healing, Thou the Abiding, O Thou Abiding One!

I call on Thee O Quencher of thirsts, O Transcendent Lord, O Most Precious One!

Thou the Sufficing, Thou the Healing, Thou the Abiding, O Thou Abiding One!

I call on Thee O Greatest Remembrance, O Noblest Name, O Most Ancient Way! Thou the Sufficing, Thou the Healing, Thou the Abiding, O Thou Abiding One!

I call on Thee O Most Lauded, O Most Holy, O Sanctified One! Thou the Sufficing, Thou the Healing, Thou the Abiding, O Thou Abiding One!

I call on Thee O Unfastener, O Counselor, O Deliverer! Thou the Sufficing, Thou the Healing, Thou the Abiding, O Thou Abiding One!

I call on Thee O Friend, O Physician, O Captivating One! Thou the Sufficing, Thou the Healing, Thou the Abiding, O Thou Abiding One!

I call on Thee O Glory, O Beauty, O Bountiful One! Thou the Sufficing, Thou the Healing, Thou the Abiding, O Thou Abiding One!

I call on Thee O the Most Trusted, O the Best Lover, O Lord of the Dawn! Thou the Sufficing, Thou the Healing, Thou the Abiding, O Thou Abiding One!

I call on Thee O Enkindler, O Brightener,
O Bringer of Delight! Thou the Sufficing, Thou
the Healing, Thou the Abiding, O Thou Abiding One!

I call on Thee O Lord of Bounty, O Most
Compassionate, O Most Merciful One! Thou
the Sufficing, Thou the Healing, Thou the
Abiding, O Thou Abiding One!

I call on Thee O Constant One, O Life-Giving One, O Source of all Being! Thou the
Sufficing, Thou the Healing, Thou the Abiding, O Thou Abiding One!

I call on Thee O Thou Who penetratest all
things, O All-Seeing God, O Lord of Utterance! Thou the Sufficing, Thou the Healing,
Thou the Abiding, O Thou Abiding One!

I call on Thee O Manifest yet Hidden, O
Unseen yet Renowned, O Onlooker sought by
all! Thou the Sufficing, Thou the Healing,
Thou the Abiding, O Thou Abiding One!

I call on Thee O Thou Who slayest the Lovers, O God of Grace to the wicked!

O Sufficer, I call on Thee, O Sufficer!

O Healer, I call on Thee, O Healer!

O Abider, I call on Thee, O Abider!

Thou the Ever-Abiding, O Thou Abiding One!

Sanctified art Thou, O my God! I beseech Thee by Thy generosity, whereby the portals of Thy bounty and grace were opened wide, whereby the Temple of Thy Holiness was established upon the throne of eternity; and by Thy mercy whereby Thou didst invite all created things unto the table of Thy bounties and bestowals; and by Thy grace whereby Thou didst respond, in Thine own Self with Thy word "Yea!" on behalf of all in heaven and earth, at the hour when Thy sovereignty and Thy grandeur stood revealed, at the dawn-time when the might of Thy dominion was made manifest. And again do I beseech Thee, by these most beauteous names, by these most noble and sublime attributes, and by Thy most Exalted Remembrance, and by Thy pure and spotless Beauty, and by Thy hidden Light in the most hidden pavilion, and by Thy Name, cloaked with the garment of affliction every morn and eve, to protect the bearer of this blessed Tablet, and whoso reciteth it, and whoso cometh upon it, and whoso passeth around the house wherein it is. Heal Thou, then, by it every sick, diseased and poor one, from every tribulation and distress, from every loathsome affliction and sorrow, and guide Thou by it whosoever desireth to enter upon the paths of Thy guidance, and the ways of Thy forgiveness and grace.

Thou art verily the Powerful, the All-Sufficing, the Healing, the Protector, the Giving, the Compassionate, the All-Generous, the All-Merciful.   —*Bahá'u'lláh*

HUMANITY

My God, Whom I worship and adore! I bear witness unto Thy unity and Thy oneness, and acknowledge Thy gifts, both in the past and in the present. Thou art the All-Bountiful, the overflowing showers of Whose mercy have rained down upon high and low alike, and the splendors of Whose grace have been shed over both the obedient and the rebellious.

O God of mercy, before Whose door the quintessence of mercy hath bowed down, and round the sanctuary of Whose Cause loving-kindness, in its inmost spirit, hath circled, we beseech Thee, entreating Thine ancient grace, and seeking Thy present favor, that Thou mayest have mercy upon all who are the manifestations of the world of being, and deny them not the outpourings of Thy grace in Thy days.

All are but poor and needy, and Thou, ver-

ily, art the All-Possessing, the All-Subduing, the
All-Powerful.   —*Bahá'u'lláh*

O Thou compassionate Lord, Thou Who
art generous and able! We are servants
of Thine sheltered beneath Thy providence.
Cast Thy glance of favor upon us. Give light
to our eyes, hearing to our ears, and understanding and love to our hearts. Render our
souls joyous and happy through Thy glad
tidings. O Lord! Point out to us the pathway
of Thy kingdom and resuscitate all of us
through the breaths of the Holy Spirit. Bestow upon us life everlasting and confer upon
us never-ending honor. Unify mankind and
illumine the world of humanity. May we all
follow Thy pathway, long for Thy good pleasure and seek the mysteries of Thy kingdom.
O God! Unite us and connect our hearts with
Thy indissoluble bond. Verily, Thou art the
Giver, Thou art the Kind One and Thou art
the Almighty.   —*'Abdu'l-Bahá*

O Thou kind Lord! O Thou Who art generous and merciful! We are the servants
of Thy threshold and are gathered beneath

the sheltering shadow of Thy divine unity.
The sun of Thy mercy is shining upon all,
and the clouds of Thy bounty shower upon
all. Thy gifts encompass all, Thy loving
providence sustains all, Thy protection over-
shadows all, and the glances of Thy favor are
cast upon all. O Lord! Grant Thine infinite
bestowals, and let the light of Thy guidance
shine. Illumine the eyes, gladden the hearts
with abiding joy. Confer a new spirit upon all
people and bestow upon them eternal life.
Unlock the gates of true understanding and
let the light of faith shine resplendent.
Gather all people beneath the shadow of Thy
bounty and cause them to unite in harmony,
so that they may become as the rays of one
sun, as the waves of one ocean, and as the
fruit of one tree. May they drink from the
same fountain. May they be refreshed by the
same breeze. May they receive illumination
from the same source of light. Thou art the
Giver, the Merciful, the Omnipotent.

—'Abdu'l-Bahá

O Thou kind Lord! Thou hast created all
humanity from the same stock. Thou

hast decreed that all shall belong to the same household. In Thy Holy Presence they are all Thy servants, and all mankind are sheltered beneath Thy Tabernacle; all have gathered together at Thy Table of Bounty; all are illumined through the light of Thy Providence.

O God! Thou art kind to all, Thou hast provided for all, dost shelter all, conferrest life upon all. Thou hast endowed each and all with talents and faculties, and all are submerged in the Ocean of Thy Mercy.

O Thou kind Lord! Unite all. Let the religions agree and make the nations one, so that they may see each other as one family and the whole earth as one home. May they all live together in perfect harmony.

O God! Raise aloft the banner of the oneness of mankind.

O God! Establish the Most Great Peace.

Cement Thou, O God, the hearts together.

O Thou kind Father, God! Gladden our hearts through the fragrance of Thy love. Brighten our eyes through the Light of Thy Guidance. Delight our ears with the melody of Thy Word, and shelter us all in the Stronghold of Thy Providence.

Thou art the Mighty and Powerful, Thou art the Forgiving and Thou art the One Who overlooketh the shortcomings of all mankind.
— *'Abdu'l-Bahá*

O God, O Thou Who hast cast Thy splendor over the luminous realities of men, shedding upon them the resplendent lights of knowledge and guidance, and hast chosen them out of all created things for this supernal grace, and hast caused them to encompass all things, to understand their inmost essence, and to disclose their mysteries, bringing them forth out of darkness into the visible world! "He verily showeth His special mercy to whomsoever He will."*

O Lord, help Thou Thy loved ones to acquire knowledge and the sciences and arts, and to unravel the secrets that are treasured up in the inmost reality of all created beings. Make them to hear the hidden truths that are written and embedded in the heart of all that is. Make them to be ensigns of guidance amongst all creatures, and piercing rays of the mind shed-

* Qur'án 3:67.

ding forth their light in this, the "first life."* Make them to be leaders unto Thee, guides unto Thy path, runners urging men on to Thy Kingdom.

Thou verily art the Powerful, the Protector, the Potent, the Defender, the Mighty, the Most Generous. —'Abdu'l-Bahá

* Qur'án 56:62.

MARRIAGE

"Bahá'í marriage is union and cordial affection between the two parties. They must, however, exercise the utmost care and become acquainted with each other's character. This eternal bond should be made secure by a firm covenant, and the intention should be to foster harmony, fellowship and unity and to attain everlasting life."
—'Abdu'l-Bahá

The pledge of marriage, the verse to be spoken individually by the bride and the bridegroom in the presence of at least two witnesses acceptable to the Spiritual Assembly is, as stipulated in the Kitáb-i-Aqdas (The Most Holy Book):

"We will all, verily, abide by the Will of God."

He is the Bestower, the Bounteous! Praise be to God, the Ancient, the Ever-Abiding, the Changeless, the Eternal! He Who hath testified in His Own Being that verily He

is the One, the Single, the Untrammeled, the
Exalted. We bear witness that verily there is no
God but Him, acknowledging His oneness,
confessing His singleness. He hath ever dwelt
in unapproachable heights, in the summits of
His loftiness, sanctified from the mention of
aught save Himself, free from the description
of aught but Him.

And when He desired to manifest grace and
beneficence to men, and to set the world in
order, He revealed observances and created
laws; among them He established the law of
marriage, made it as a fortress for well-being
and salvation, and enjoined it upon us in that
which was sent down out of the heaven of sanctity in His Most Holy Book. He saith, great is
His glory: "Enter into wedlock, O people, that
ye may bring forth one who will make mention of Me amid My servants. This is My bidding unto you; hold fast to it as an assistance
to yourselves."   —*Bahá'u'lláh*

He is God!
O peerless Lord! In Thine almighty wisdom Thou hast enjoined marriage upon the

peoples, that the generations of men may succeed one another in this contingent world, and that ever, so long as the world shall last, they may busy themselves at the Threshold of Thy oneness with servitude and worship, with salutation, adoration and praise. "I have not created spirits and men, but that they should worship me."* Wherefore, wed Thou in the heaven of Thy mercy these two birds of the nest of Thy love, and make them the means of attracting perpetual grace; that from the union of these two seas of love a wave of tenderness may surge and cast the pearls of pure and goodly issue on the shore of life. "He hath let loose the two seas, that they meet each other: Between them is a barrier which they overpass not. Which then of the bounties of your Lord will ye deny? From each He bringeth up greater and lesser pearls."†

O Thou kind Lord! Make Thou this marriage to bring forth coral and pearls. Thou art

* Qur'án 51:56.
† Qur'án 55:19–22.

verily the All-Powerful, the Most Great, the
Ever-Forgiving.   —'Abdu'l-Bahá

Glory be unto Thee, O my God! Verily,
this Thy servant and this Thy maidservant have gathered under the shadow of Thy
mercy and they are united through Thy favor
and generosity. O Lord! Assist them in this
Thy world and Thy kingdom and destine for
them every good through Thy bounty and
grace. O Lord! Confirm them in Thy servitude and assist them in Thy service. Suffer
them to become the signs of Thy Name in
Thy world and protect them through Thy
bestowals which are inexhaustible in this
world and the world to come. O Lord! They
are supplicating the kingdom of Thy mercifulness and invoking the realm of Thy singleness. Verily, they are married in obedience
to Thy command. Cause them to become the
signs of harmony and unity until the end of
time. Verily, Thou art the Omnipotent, the
Omnipresent and the Almighty!

          —'Abdu'l-Bahá

O my Lord, O my Lord! These two bright orbs are wedded in Thy love, conjoined in servitude to Thy Holy Threshold, united in ministering to Thy Cause. Make Thou this marriage to be as threading lights of Thine abounding grace, O my Lord, the All-Merciful, and luminous rays of Thy bestowals, O Thou the Beneficent, the Ever-Giving, that there may branch out from this great tree boughs that will grow green and flourishing through the gifts that rain down from Thy clouds of grace.

Verily, Thou art the Generous. Verily, Thou art the Almighty. Verily, Thou art the Compassionate, the All-Merciful.   — 'Abdu'l-Bahá

MORNING

O my God and my Master! I am Thy servant and the son of Thy servant. I have risen from my couch at this dawntide when the Daystar of Thy oneness hath shone forth from the Dayspring of Thy will, and hath shed its radiance upon the whole world, according to what had been ordained in the Books of Thy Decree.

Praise be unto Thee, O my God, that we have wakened to the splendors of the light of Thy knowledge. Send down, then, upon us, O my Lord, what will enable us to dispense with anyone but Thee, and will rid us of all attachment to aught except Thyself. Write down, moreover, for me, and for such as are dear to me, and for my kindred, man and woman alike, the good of this world and the world to come. Keep us safe, then, through Thine unfailing protection, O Thou the Beloved of the entire creation and the Desire of the whole universe, from them whom Thou hast made to be the manifestations of the Evil Whisperer, who whisper in men's breasts. Potent art Thou to do Thy pleasure. Thou art, verily, the Almighty, the Help in Peril, the Self-Subsisting.

Bless Thou, O Lord my God, Him Whom Thou hast set over Thy most excellent Titles, and through Whom Thou hast divided between the godly and the wicked, and graciously aid us to do what Thou lovest and desirest. Bless Thou, moreover, O my God, them Who are Thy Words and Thy Letters, and them who have set their faces towards Thee, and turned unto Thy face, and hearkened to Thy Call.

Thou art, truly, the Lord and King of all men, and art potent over all things.

— *Bahá'u'lláh*

I have wakened in Thy shelter, O my God, and it becometh him that seeketh that shelter to abide within the Sanctuary of Thy protection and the Stronghold of Thy defense. Illumine my inner being, O my Lord, with the splendors of the Dayspring of Thy

Revelation, even as Thou didst illumine my outer being with the morning light of Thy favor.   —*Bahá'u'lláh*

I have risen this morning by Thy grace, O my God, and left my home trusting wholly in Thee, and committing myself to Thy care. Send down, then, upon me, out of the heaven of Thy mercy, a blessing from Thy side, and enable me to return home in safety even as Thou didst enable me to set out under Thy protection with my thoughts fixed steadfastly upon Thee.

There is none other God but Thee, the One, the Incomparable, the All-Knowing, the All-Wise.   —*Bahá'u'lláh*

I give praise to Thee, O my God, that Thou hast awakened me out of my sleep, and brought me forth after my disappearance, and raised me up from my slumber. I have wakened this morning with my face set toward the splendors of the Daystar of Thy Revelation, through Which the heavens of Thy power and Thy majesty have been illumined, acknowledging Thy signs, believing in Thy Book, and holding fast unto Thy Cord.

I beseech Thee, by the potency of Thy will and the compelling power of Thy purpose, to make of what Thou didst reveal unto me in my sleep the surest foundation for the mansions of Thy love that are within the hearts of Thy loved ones, and the best instrument for the revelation of the tokens of Thy grace and Thy loving-kindness.

Do Thou ordain for me through Thy most exalted Pen, O my Lord, the good of this world and of the next. I testify that within Thy grasp are held the reins of all things. Thou changest them as Thou pleasest. No God is there save Thee, the Strong, the Faithful.

Thou art He Who changeth through His bidding abasement into glory, and weakness into strength, and powerlessness into might, and fear into calm, and doubt into certainty. No God is there but Thee, the Mighty, the Beneficent.

Thou disappointest no one who hath sought Thee, nor dost Thou keep back from Thee anyone who hath desired Thee. Ordain Thou for me what becometh the heaven of Thy generosity, and the ocean of Thy bounty. Thou art, verily, the Almighty, the Most Powerful.

—*Bahá'u'lláh*

NEARNESS TO GOD

Glory be to Thee, O my God! Thou hearest Thine ardent lovers lamenting in their separation from Thee, and such as have recognized Thee wailing because of their remoteness from Thy presence. Open Thou outwardly to their faces, O my Lord, the gates of Thy grace, that they may enter them by Thy leave and in conformity with Thy will, and may stand before the throne of Thy majesty, and catch the accents of Thy voice, and be illumined with the splendors of the light of Thy face.

Potent art Thou to do what pleaseth Thee. None can withstand the power of Thy sovereign might. From everlasting Thou wert alone, with none to equal Thee, and wilt unto everlasting remain far above all thought and every description of Thee. Have mercy, then, upon Thy servants by Thy grace and bounty, and

suffer them not to be kept back from the shores
of the ocean of Thy nearness. If Thou
abandonest them, who is there to befriend
them; and if Thou puttest them far from Thee,
who is he that can favor them? They have none
other Lord beside Thee, none to adore except
Thyself. Deal Thou generously with them by
Thy bountiful grace.

Thou, in truth, art the Ever-Forgiving, the
Most Compassionate.   —*Bahá'u'lláh*

Verily I am Thy servant, O my God, and
Thy poor one and Thy suppliant and
Thy wretched creature. I have arrived at Thy
gate, seeking Thy shelter. I have found no
contentment save in Thy love, no exultation
except in Thy remembrance, no eagerness
but in obedience to Thee, no joy save in Thy
nearness, and no tranquillity except in reunion with Thee, notwithstanding that I am
conscious that all created things are debarred
from Thy sublime Essence and the entire creation is denied access to Thine inmost Being.
Whenever I attempt to approach Thee, I perceive nothing in myself but the tokens of

Thy grace and behold naught in my being but the revelations of Thy loving-kindness. How can one who is but Thy creature seek reunion with Thee and attain unto Thy presence, whereas no created thing can ever be associated with Thee, nor can aught comprehend Thee? How is it possible for a lowly servant to recognize Thee and to extol Thy praise, notwithstanding that Thou hast destined for him the revelations of Thy dominion and the wondrous testimonies of Thy sovereignty? Thus every created thing beareth witness that it is debarred from the sanctuary of Thy presence by reason of the limitations imposed upon its inner reality. It is undisputed, however, that the influence of Thine attraction hath everlastingly been inherent in the realities of Thy handiwork, although that which beseemeth the hallowed court of Thy providence is exalted beyond the attainment of the entire creation. This indicateth, O my God, my utter powerlessness to praise Thee and revealeth my utmost impotence in yielding thanks unto Thee; and how much more to attain the recognition of

Thy divine unity or to succeed in reaching
the clear tokens of Thy praise, Thy sanctity
and Thy glory. Nay, by Thy might, I yearn
for naught but Thine Own Self and seek no
one other than Thee.   — *The Báb*

O my God! There is no one but Thee to
allay the anguish of my soul, and Thou
art my highest aspiration, O my God. My
heart is wedded to none save Thee and such
as Thou dost love. I solemnly declare that my
life and death are both for Thee. Verily Thou
art incomparable and hast no partner.

O my Lord! I beg Thee to forgive me for shut-
ting myself out from Thee. By Thy glory and
majesty, I have failed to befittingly recognize
Thee and to worship Thee, while Thou dost
make Thyself known unto me and callest me
to remembrance as beseemeth Thy station.
Grievous woe would betide me, O my Lord,
wert Thou to take hold of me by reason of my
misdeeds and trespasses. No helper do I know
of other than Thee. No refuge do I have to flee
to save Thee. None among Thy creatures can

dare to intercede with Thyself without Thy leave. I hold fast to Thy love before Thy court, and, according to Thy bidding, I earnestly pray unto Thee as befitteth Thy glory. I beg Thee to heed my call as Thou hast promised me. Verily Thou art God; no God is there but Thee. Alone and unaided, Thou art independent of all created things. Neither can the devotion of Thy lovers profit Thee, nor the evil doings of the faithless harm Thee. Verily Thou art my God, He Who will never fail in His promise.

O my God! I beseech Thee by the evidences of Thy favor, to let me draw nigh to the sublime heights of Thy holy presence, and protect me from inclining myself toward the subtle allusions of aught else but Thee. Guide my steps, O my God, unto that which is acceptable and pleasing to Thee. Shield me, through Thy might, from the fury of Thy wrath and chastisement, and hold me back from entering habitations not desired by Thee.   *— The Báb*

O God, my God, my Beloved, my heart's Desire.   *— The Báb*

O Lord, my God and my Haven in my distress! My Shield and my Shelter in my woes! My Asylum and Refuge in time of need and in my loneliness my Companion! In my anguish my Solace, and in my solitude a loving Friend! The Remover of the pangs of my sorrows and the Pardoner of my sins!

Wholly unto Thee do I turn, fervently imploring Thee with all my heart, my mind and my tongue, to shield me from all that runs counter to Thy will in this, the cycle of Thy divine unity, and to cleanse me of all defilement that will hinder me from seeking, stainless and unsullied, the shade of the tree of Thy grace.

Have mercy, O Lord, on the feeble, make whole the sick, and quench the burning thirst.

Gladden the bosom wherein the fire of Thy love doth smolder, and set it aglow with the flame of Thy celestial love and spirit.

Robe the tabernacles of divine unity with the vesture of holiness, and set upon my head the crown of Thy favor.

Illumine my face with the radiance of the orb of Thy bounty, and graciously aid me in ministering at Thy holy threshold.

Make my heart overflow with love for Thy creatures and grant that I may become the sign of Thy mercy, the token of Thy grace, the promoter of concord amongst Thy loved ones, devoted unto Thee, uttering Thy commemoration and forgetful of self but ever mindful of what is Thine.

O God, my God! Stay not from me the gentle gales of Thy pardon and grace, and deprive me not of the wellsprings of Thine aid and favor.

'Neath the shade of Thy protecting wings let me nestle, and cast upon me the glance of Thine all-protecting eye.

Loose my tongue to laud Thy name amidst Thy people, that my voice may be raised in great assemblies and from my lips may stream the flood of Thy praise.

Thou art, in all truth, the Gracious, the Glorified, the Mighty, the Omnipotent.

— 'Abdu'l-Bahá

He is the Compassionate, the All-Bountiful! O God, my God! Thou seest me, Thou knowest me; Thou art my Haven and my Refuge. None have I sought nor any will I seek save Thee; no path have I trodden nor any will I tread but the path of Thy love. In the darksome night of despair, my eye turneth expectant and full of hope to the morn of Thy boundless favor and at the hour of dawn my drooping soul is refreshed and strengthened in remembrance of Thy beauty and perfection. He whom the grace of Thy mercy aideth, though he be but a drop, shall become the boundless ocean, and the merest atom which the outpouring of Thy lovingkindness assisteth, shall shine even as the radiant star.

Shelter under Thy protection, O Thou Spirit of purity, Thou Who art the All-Bountiful Provider, this enthralled, enkindled servant of Thine. Aid him in this world of being to remain steadfast and firm in Thy love and grant that this broken-winged bird attain a refuge and shelter in Thy divine nest that abideth upon the celestial tree.   —'Abdu'l-Bahá

PRAISE AND GRATITUDE

All praise, O my God, be to Thee Who art the Source of all glory and majesty, of greatness and honor, of sovereignty and dominion, of loftiness and grace, of awe and power. Whomsoever Thou willest Thou causest to draw nigh unto the Most Great Ocean, and on whomsoever Thou desirest Thou conferrest the honor of recognizing Thy Most Ancient Name. Of all who are in heaven and on earth, none can withstand the operation of Thy sovereign Will. From all eternity Thou didst rule the entire creation, and Thou wilt continue for evermore to exercise Thy dominion over all created things. There is none other God but Thee, the Almighty, the Most Exalted, the All-Powerful, the All-Wise.

Illumine, O Lord, the faces of Thy servants, that they may behold Thee; and cleanse their hearts that they may turn unto the court of Thy heavenly favors, and recognize Him Who is the Manifestation of Thy Self and the Dayspring of Thine Essence. Verily, Thou art the Lord of all worlds. There is no God but Thee, the Unconstrained, the All-Subduing.

—*Bahá'u'lláh*

In the Name of God, the Most High! Lauded and glorified art Thou, Lord, God Omnipotent! Thou before Whose wisdom the wise falleth short and faileth, before Whose knowledge the learned confesseth his ignorance, before Whose might the strong waxeth weak, before Whose wealth the rich testifieth to his poverty, before Whose light the enlightened is lost in darkness, toward the shrine of Whose knowledge turneth the essence of all understanding and around the sanctuary of Whose presence circle the souls of all mankind.

How then can I sing and tell of Thine Essence, which the wisdom of the wise and the learning of the learned have failed to comprehend, inasmuch as no man can sing that which he understandeth not, nor recount that unto which he cannot attain, whilst Thou hast been from everlasting the Inaccessible, the Unsearchable. Powerless though I be to rise to the heavens of Thy glory and soar in the realms of Thy knowledge, I can but recount Thy tokens that tell of Thy glorious handiwork.

By Thy Glory! O Beloved of all hearts, Thou that alone canst still the pangs of yearning for Thee! Though all the dwellers of heaven and earth unite to glorify the least of Thy signs, wherein and whereby Thou hast revealed Thyself, yet would they fail, how much more to praise Thy holy Word, the creator of all Thy tokens.

All praise and glory be to Thee, Thou of Whom all things have testified that Thou art one and there is none other God but Thee, Who hast been from everlasting exalted above all peer or likeness and to everlasting shalt remain the same. All kings are but Thy servants and all beings, visible and invisible, as naught before Thee. There is none other God but Thee, the Gracious, the Powerful, the Most High.

—Bahá'u'lláh

Magnified be Thy name, O Lord my God! Thou art He Whom all things worship and Who worshipeth no one, Who is the Lord of all things and is the vassal of none, Who knoweth all things and is known of none. Thou didst wish to make Thyself known unto men; therefore, Thou didst, through a word of Thy mouth, bring creation into being and fashion the universe. There is none other God except Thee, the Fashioner, the Creator, the Almighty, the Most Powerful.

I implore Thee, by this very word that hath shone forth above the horizon of Thy will, to enable me to drink deep of the living waters through which Thou hast vivified the hearts of Thy chosen ones and quickened the souls of them that love Thee, that I may, at all times and under all conditions, turn my face wholly towards Thee.

Thou art the God of power, of glory and

bounty. No God is there beside Thee, the Supreme Ruler, the All-Glorious, the Omniscient.
— *Bahá'u'lláh*

Glorified art Thou, O Lord my God! I yield Thee thanks for having enabled me to recognize the Manifestation of Thyself, and for having severed me from Thine enemies, and laid bare before mine eyes their misdeeds and wicked works in Thy days, and for having rid me of all attachment to them, and caused me to turn wholly towards Thy grace and bountiful favors. I give Thee thanks, also, for having sent down upon me from the clouds of Thy will that which hath so sanctified me from the hints of the infidels and the allusions of the misbelievers that I have fixed my heart firmly on Thee, and fled from such as have denied the light of Thy countenance. Again I thank Thee for having empowered me to be steadfast in Thy love, and to speak forth Thy praise and to extol Thy virtues, and for having given me to drink of the cup of Thy mercy that hath surpassed all things visible and invisible.

Thou art the Almighty, the Most Exalted, the All-Glorious, the All-Loving.

—*Bahá'u'lláh*

Praised be Thou, O Lord my God! Every time I attempt to make mention of Thee, I am hindered by the sublimity of Thy station and the overpowering greatness of Thy might. For were I to praise Thee throughout the length of Thy dominion and the duration of Thy sovereignty, I would find that my praise of Thee can befit only such as are like unto me, who are themselves Thy creatures, and who have been generated through the power of Thy decree and been fashioned through the potency of Thy will. And at whatever time my pen ascribeth glory to any one of Thy names, methinks I can hear the voice of its lamentation in its remoteness from Thee, and can recognize its cry because of its separation from Thy Self. I testify that everything other than Thee is but Thy creation and is held in the hollow of Thy hand. To have accepted any act or praise from Thy creatures is but an evidence of the wonders of Thy grace and bountiful favors, and a manifestation of Thy generosity and providence.

I entreat Thee, O my Lord, by Thy Most Great Name whereby Thou didst separate light from fire, and truth from denial, to send down upon me and upon such of my loved ones as are in my company the good of this world and of the next. Supply us, then, with Thy wondrous gifts that are hid from the eyes of men. Thou art, verily, the Fashioner of all creation. No God is there but Thee, the Almighty, the All-Glorious, the Most High. —*Bahá'u'lláh*

All majesty and glory, O my God, and all dominion and light and grandeur and splendor be unto Thee. Thou bestowest sovereignty on whom Thou willest and dost withhold it from whom Thou desirest. No God is there but Thee, the All-Possessing, the Most Exalted. Thou art He Who createth from naught the universe and all that dwell therein. There is nothing worthy of Thee except Thyself, while all else but Thee are as outcasts in Thy holy presence and are as nothing when compared to the glory of Thine Own Being.

Far be it from me to extol Thy virtues save by what Thou hast extolled Thyself in Thy weighty Book where Thou sayest, "No vision taketh in Him, but He taketh in all vision. He is the Subtile, the All-Perceiving."* Glory be unto Thee, O my God, indeed no mind or vision, however keen or discriminating, can ever grasp the nature of the most insignificant of Thy signs. Verily, Thou art God, no God is there besides Thee. I bear witness that Thou Thyself alone art the sole expression of Thine attributes, that the praise of no one besides Thee can ever attain to Thy holy court nor can Thine attributes ever be fathomed by anyone other than Thyself.

Glory be unto Thee, Thou art exalted above the description of anyone save Thyself, since it is beyond human conception to befittingly magnify Thy virtues or to comprehend the inmost reality of Thine Essence. Far be it from Thy glory that Thy creatures should describe

* Qur'án 6:103.

Thee or that anyone besides Thyself should ever know Thee. I have known Thee, O my God, by reason of Thy making Thyself known unto me, for hadst Thou not revealed Thyself unto me, I would not have known Thee. I worship Thee by virtue of Thy summoning me unto Thee, for had it not been for Thy summons I would not have worshiped Thee.

— *The Báb*

PROTECTION

Praise be to Thee, O Lord my God! Thou seest and knowest that I have called upon Thy servants to turn nowhere except in the direction of Thy bestowals, and have bidden them observe naught save the things Thou didst prescribe in Thy Perspicuous Book, the Book which hath been sent down according to Thine inscrutable decree and irrevocable purpose.

I can utter no word, O my God, unless I be permitted by Thee, and can move in no direction until I obtain Thy sanction. It is Thou, O my God, Who hast called me into being through the power of Thy might, and hast endued me with Thy grace to manifest Thy Cause. Wherefore I have been subjected to such adversities that my tongue hath been hindered from extolling Thee and from magnifying Thy glory.

All praise be to Thee, O my God, for the things Thou didst ordain for me through Thy decree and by the power of Thy sovereignty. I beseech Thee that Thou wilt fortify both myself and them that love me in our love for Thee, and wilt keep us firm in Thy Cause. I swear by Thy might! O my God! Thy servant's shame is to be shut out as by a veil from Thee, and his glory is to know Thee. Armed with the power of Thy name nothing can ever hurt me, and with Thy love in my heart all the world's afflictions can in no wise alarm me.

Send down, therefore, O my Lord, upon me and upon my loved ones that which will protect us from the mischief of those that have repudiated Thy truth and disbelieved in Thy signs.

Thou art, verily, the All-Glorious, the Most Bountiful.   —*Bahá'u'lláh*

Praised be Thou, O Lord my God! This is Thy servant who hath quaffed from the hands of Thy grace the wine of Thy tender mercy, and tasted of the savor of Thy love in Thy days. I beseech Thee, by the embodiments of Thy names whom no grief can hinder from rejoicing in Thy love or from gazing on Thy face, and whom all the hosts of the heedless are powerless to cause to turn aside from the path of Thy pleasure, to supply him with the good things Thou dost possess, and to raise him up to such heights that he will regard the world even as a shadow that vanisheth swifter than the twinkling of an eye.

Keep him safe also, O my God, by the power of Thine immeasurable majesty, from all that Thou abhorrest. Thou art, verily, his Lord and the Lord of all worlds.   —*Bahá'u'lláh*

Lauded be Thy name, O Lord my God! I entreat Thee by Thy Name through which the Hour hath struck, and the Resurrection came to pass, and fear and trembling seized all that are in heaven and all that are on earth, to rain down, out of the heaven of Thy mercy and the clouds of Thy tender compassion, what will gladden the hearts of Thy servants, who have turned towards Thee and helped Thy Cause.

Keep safe Thy servants and Thy handmaidens, O my Lord, from the darts of idle fancy and vain imaginings, and give them from the hands of Thy grace a draught of the soft-flowing waters of Thy knowledge.

Thou, truly, art the Almighty, the Most Exalted, the Ever-Forgiving, the Most Generous.

—*Bahá'u'lláh*

O God, my God! I have set out from my home, holding fast unto the cord of Thy love, and I have committed myself wholly to Thy care and Thy protection. I entreat Thee by Thy power through which Thou didst protect Thy loved ones from the wayward and the perverse, and from every contumacious oppressor, and every wicked doer who hath strayed far from Thee, to keep me safe by Thy bounty and Thy grace. Enable me, then, to return to my home by Thy power and Thy might. Thou art, truly, the Almighty, the Help in Peril, the Self-Subsisting.

—*Bahá'u'lláh*

In His Name, the Exalted, the All-Highest, the Most Sublime!

Glorified art Thou, O Lord my God! O Thou Who art my God, and my Master, and my Lord, and my Support, and my Hope, and my Refuge, and my Light. I ask of Thee, by Thy Hidden and Treasured Name, which none knoweth save Thine own Self, to protect the bearer of this Tablet from every calamity and pestilence, and from every wicked man and woman; from the evil of the evil-doers, and from the scheming of the unbelievers. Preserve him, moreover, O my God, from every pain and vexation, O Thou Who holdest in Thy hand the empire of all things. Thou, truly, art powerful over all things. Thou doest as Thou willest, and ordainest as Thou pleasest.

O Thou King of Kings! O Thou kind Lord! O Thou Source of ancient bounty, of grace, of generosity and bestowal! O Thou Healer of sicknesses! O Thou Sufficer of needs! O Thou Light of Light! O Thou Light above all Lights! O Thou Revealer of every Manifestation! O Thou the Compassionate! O Thou the Merciful! Do Thou have mercy upon the bearer of this Tablet, through Thy most great mercy and Thine abundant grace, O Thou the Gracious, Thou the Bounteous. Guard him, moreover, through Thy protection, from whatsoever his heart and mind may find repugnant. Of those endued with power, Thou, verily, art the most powerful. The Glory of God rest upon thee, O thou rising sun! Do thou testify unto that which God hath testified of His own Self, that there is none other God besides Him, the Almighty, the Best-Beloved. —*Bahá'u'lláh*

Ordain for me, O my Lord, and for those who believe in Thee that which is deemed best for us in Thine estimation, as set forth in the Mother Book, for within the grasp of Thy hand Thou holdest the determined measures of all things.

Thy goodly gifts are unceasingly showered upon such as cherish Thy love, and the wondrous tokens of Thy heavenly bounties are amply bestowed on those who recognize Thy divine Unity. We commit unto Thy care whatsoever Thou hast destined for us, and implore

Thee to grant us all the good that Thy knowledge embraceth.

Protect me, O my Lord, from every evil that Thine omniscience perceiveth, inasmuch as there is no power nor strength but in Thee, no triumph is forthcoming save from Thy presence, and it is Thine alone to command. Whatever God hath willed hath been, and that which He hath not willed shall not be.

There is no power nor strength except in God, the Most Exalted, the Most Mighty.

— *The Báb*

Glory be to Thee, O God! Thou art the God Who hath existed before all things, Who will exist after all things and will last beyond all things. Thou art the God Who knoweth all things, and is supreme over all things. Thou art the God Who dealeth mercifully with all things, Who judgeth between all things and Whose vision embraceth all things. Thou art God my Lord, Thou art aware of my position, Thou dost witness my inner and outer being.

Grant Thy forgiveness unto me and unto the

believers who responded to Thy Call. Be Thou
my sufficing helper against the mischief of
whosoever may desire to inflict sorrow upon me
or wish me ill. Verily, Thou art the Lord of all
created things. Thou dost suffice everyone,
while no one can be self-sufficient without
Thee. — *The Báb*

In the Name of God, the Lord of overpowering majesty, the All-Compelling.

Hallowed be the Lord in Whose hand is the
source of dominion. He createth whatsoever He
willeth by His Word of command "Be," and it
is. His hath been the power of authority here-
tofore, and it shall remain His hereafter. He
maketh victorious whomsoever He pleaseth,
through the potency of His behest. He is in
truth the Powerful, the Almighty. Unto Him
pertaineth all glory and majesty in the kingdoms of Revelation and Creation and whatever lieth between them. Verily, He is the Potent, the All-Glorious. From everlasting He
hath been the Source of indomitable strength
and shall remain so unto everlasting. He is indeed the Lord of might and power. All the king-

doms of heaven and earth and whatever is between them are God's, and His power is supreme over all things. All the treasures of earth and heaven and everything between them are His, and His protection extendeth over all things. He is the Creator of the heavens and the earth and whatever lieth between them, and He truly is a witness over all things. He is the Lord of Reckoning for all that dwell in the heavens and on earth and whatever lieth between them, and truly God is swift to reckon. He setteth the measure assigned to all who are in the heavens and the earth and whatever is between them. Verily, He is the Supreme Protector. He holdeth in His grasp the keys of heaven and earth and of everything between them. At His Own pleasure doth He bestow gifts, through the power of His command. Indeed His grace encompasseth all, and He is the All-Knowing.

Say: God sufficeth unto me; He is the One Who holdeth in His grasp the kingdom of all things. Through the power of His hosts of heaven and earth and whatever lieth between them, He protecteth whomsoever among His servants He willeth. God, in truth, keepeth watch over all things.

Immeasurably exalted art Thou, O Lord! Protect us from what lieth in front of us and behind us, above our heads, on our right, on our left, below our feet and every other side to which we are exposed. Verily, Thy protection over all things is unfailing.*   — *The Báb*

O God, my God! Shield Thy trusted servants from the evils of self and passion, protect them with the watchful eye of Thy loving-kindness from all rancor, hate and envy, shelter them in the impregnable stronghold of Thy care and, safe from the darts of doubtfulness, make them the manifestations of Thy glorious signs, illumine their faces with the effulgent rays shed from the Dayspring of Thy divine unity, gladden their hearts with the verses revealed from Thy holy kingdom, strengthen their loins by Thine all-swaying power that cometh from

---

* The original of this prayer for protection is written in the Báb's own hand, in the form of a pentacle.

Thy realm of glory. Thou art the All-Bountiful, the Protector, the Almighty, the Gracious.   — 'Abdu'l-Bahá

O my Lord! Thou knowest that the people
are encircled with pain and calamities
and are environed with hardships and
trouble. Every trial doth attack man and every dire adversity doth assail him like unto
the assault of a serpent. There is no shelter
and asylum for him except under the wing of
Thy protection, preservation, guard and custody.

   O Thou the Merciful One! O my Lord! Make
Thy protection my armor, Thy preservation my
shield, humbleness before the door of Thy oneness my guard, and Thy custody and defense
my fortress and my abode. Preserve me from
the suggestions of self and desire, and guard
me from every sickness, trial, difficulty and
ordeal.

   Verily, Thou art the Protector, the Guardian, the Preserver, the Sufficer, and verily, Thou
art the Merciful of the Most Merciful.
                                    — 'Abdu'l-Bahá

O Thou kind and loving Providence! The east is astir and the west surgeth even as the eternal billows of the sea. The gentle breezes of holiness are diffused and, from the Unseen Kingdom, the rays of the Orb of Truth shine forth resplendent. The anthems of divine unity are being chanted and the ensigns of celestial might are waving. The angelic Voice is raised and, even as the roaring of the leviathan, soundeth the call to selflessness and evanescence. The triumphal cry *Yá Bahá'u'l-Abhá* resoundeth on every side, and the call *Yá 'Alíyyu'l-'Alá** ringeth throughout all regions. No stir is there in the world save that of the Glory of the One Ravisher of Hearts, and no tumult is there save the surging of the love of Him, the Incomparable, the Well-Beloved.

The beloved of the Lord, with their musk-scented breath, burn like bright candles in every clime, and the friends of the All-Merciful, even as unfolding flowers, can be found in all

---

* O Thou the Exalted, the Most Exalted!

regions. Not for a moment do they rest; they breathe not but in remembrance of Thee, and crave naught but to serve Thy Cause. In the meadows of truth they are as sweet-singing nightingales, and in the flower garden of guidance they are even as brightly-colored blossoms. With mystic flowers they adorn the walks of the Garden of Reality; as swaying cypresses they line the riverbanks of the Divine Will. Above the horizon of being they shine as radiant stars; in the firmament of the world they gleam as resplendent orbs. Manifestations of celestial grace are they, and daysprings of the light of divine assistance.

Grant, O Thou Loving Lord, that all may stand firm and steadfast, shining with everlasting splendor, so that, at every breath, gentle breezes may blow from the bowers of Thy loving-kindness, that from the ocean of Thy grace a mist may rise, that the kindly showers of Thy love may bestow freshness, and the zephyr waft its perfume from the rose garden of divine unity.

Vouchsafe, O Best Beloved of the World, a ray from Thy Splendor. O Well-Beloved of mankind, shed upon us the light of Thy Countenance.

O God Omnipotent, do Thou shield us and be our refuge and, O Lord of Being, show forth Thy might and Thy dominion.

O Thou loving Lord, the movers of sedition are in some regions astir and active, and by night and day are inflicting a grievous wrong.

Even as wolves, tyrants are lying in wait, and the wronged, innocent flock hath neither help nor succor. Hounds are on the trail of the gazelles of the fields of divine unity, and the pheasant in the mountains of heavenly guidance is pursued by the ravens of envy.

O Thou divine Providence, preserve and protect us! O Thou Who art our Shield, save us and defend us! Keep us beneath Thy Shelter, and by Thy Help save us from all ills. Thou art, indeed, the True Protector, the Unseen Guardian, the Celestial Preserver, and the Heavenly Loving Lord.   —'Abdu'l-Bahá

SERVICE

O God, and the God of all Names, and Maker of the heavens! I entreat Thee by Thy Name through which He Who is the Dayspring of Thy might and the Dawning-Place of Thy power hath been manifested, through which every solid thing hath been made to flow, and every dead corpse hath been quickened, and every moving spirit confirmed—I entreat Thee to enable me to rid myself of all attachment to any one but Thee, and to serve Thy Cause, and to wish what Thou didst wish through the power of Thy sovereignty, and to perform what is the good pleasure of Thy will.

I beseech Thee, moreover, O my God, to ordain for me what will make me rich enough to dispense with any one save Thee. Thou seest me, O my God, with my face turned towards Thee, and my hands clinging to the cord of

Thy grace. Send down upon me Thy mercy, and write down for me what Thou hast written down for Thy chosen ones. Powerful art Thou to do what pleaseth Thee. No God is there but Thee, the Ever-Forgiving, the All-Bountiful.

—*Bahá'u'lláh*

I give praise to Thee, O my God, that the fragrance of Thy loving-kindness hath enraptured me, and the gentle winds of Thy mercy have inclined me in the direction of Thy bountiful favors. Make me to quaff, O my Lord, from the fingers of Thy bounteousness the living waters which have enabled every one that hath partaken of them to rid himself of all attachment to any one save Thee, and to soar into the atmosphere of detachment from all Thy creatures, and to fix his gaze upon Thy loving providence and Thy manifold gifts.

Make me ready, in all circumstances, O my Lord, to serve Thee and to set myself towards the adored sanctuary of Thy Revelation and of Thy Beauty. If it be Thy pleasure, make me to grow as a tender herb in the meadows of Thy grace, that the gentle winds of Thy will may stir me up and bend me into conformity with Thy pleasure, in such wise that my movement and my stillness may be wholly directed by Thee.

Thou art He, by Whose name the Hidden Secret was divulged, and the Well-Guarded Name was revealed, and the seals of the sealed-up Goblet were opened, shedding thereby its fragrance over all creation, whether of the past or of the future. He who was athirst, O my Lord, hath hasted to attain the living waters of Thy grace, and the wretched creature hath yearned to immerse himself beneath the ocean of Thy riches.

I swear by Thy glory, O Lord the Beloved of the world and the Desire of all them that have recognized Thee! I am sore afflicted by the grief of my separation from Thee, in the days when the Daystar of Thy presence hath shed its radiance upon Thy people. Write down, then, for me the recompense decreed for such as have gazed on Thy face and have, by Thy leave, gained admittance into the court of Thy throne, and have, at Thy bidding, met Thee face to face.

I implore Thee, O my Lord, by Thy name the splendors of which have encompassed the earth and the heavens, to enable me so to surrender my will to what Thou hast decreed in Thy Tablets, that I may cease to discover within me any desire except what Thou didst desire through the power of Thy sovereignty, and any will save what Thou didst destine for me by Thy will.

Whither shall I turn, O my God, powerless as I am to discover any other way except the way Thou didst set before Thy chosen Ones? All the atoms of the earth proclaim Thee to be God, and testify that there is none other God besides Thee. Thou hast from eternity been powerful to do what Thou hast willed, and to ordain what Thou hast pleased.

Do Thou destine for me, O my God, what will set me, at all times, towards Thee, and enable me to cleave continually to the cord of Thy grace, and to proclaim Thy name, and to look for whatsoever may flow down from Thy pen. I am poor and desolate, O my Lord, and

Thou art the All-Possessing, the Most High. Have pity, then, upon me through the wonders of Thy mercy, and send down upon me, every moment of my life, the things wherewith Thou hast recreated the hearts of all Thy creatures who have recognized Thy unity, and of all Thy people who are wholly devoted to Thee.

Thou, verily, art the Almighty, the Most Exalted, the All-Knowing, the All-Wise.

—*Bahá'u'lláh*

SPIRITUAL GROWTH

From the sweet-scented streams of Thine eternity give me to drink, O my God, and of the fruits of the tree of Thy being enable me to taste, O my Hope! From the crystal springs of Thy love suffer me to quaff, O my Glory, and beneath the shadow of Thine everlasting providence let me abide, O my Light! Within the meadows of Thy nearness, before Thy presence, make me able to roam, O my Beloved, and at the right hand of the throne of Thy mercy, seat me, O my Desire! From the fragrant breezes of Thy joy let a breath pass over me, O my Goal, and into the heights of the paradise of Thy reality let me gain admission, O my Adored One! To the melodies of the dove of Thy oneness suffer me to hearken, O Resplendent One, and through the spirit of Thy power and Thy might quicken me, O my Provider! In the

spirit of Thy love keep me steadfast, O my
Succorer, and in the path of Thy good pleasure set firm my steps, O my Maker! Within
the garden of Thine immortality, before Thy
countenance, let me abide for ever, O Thou
Who art merciful unto me, and upon the seat
of Thy glory stablish me, O Thou Who art
my Possessor! To the heaven of Thy loving-
kindness lift me up, O my Quickener, and
unto the Daystar of Thy guidance lead me,
O Thou my Attractor! Before the revelations
of Thine invisible spirit summon me to be
present, O Thou Who art my Origin and my
Highest Wish, and unto the essence of the
fragrance of Thy beauty, which Thou wilt
manifest, cause me to return, O Thou Who
art my God!

Potent art Thou to do what pleaseth Thee.
Thou art, verily, the Most Exalted, the All-Glorious, the All-Highest.   —*Bahá'u'lláh*

Create in me a pure heart, O my God, and
renew a tranquil conscience within me,
O my Hope! Through the spirit of power

confirm Thou me in Thy Cause, O my Best-
Beloved, and by the light of Thy glory reveal
unto me Thy path, O Thou the Goal of my
desire! Through the power of Thy transcendent might lift me up unto the heaven of
Thy holiness, O Source of my being, and by
the breezes of Thine eternity gladden me, O
Thou Who art my God! Let Thine everlasting melodies breathe tranquillity on me, O
my Companion, and let the riches of Thine
ancient countenance deliver me from all except Thee, O my Master, and let the tidings
of the revelation of Thine incorruptible Essence bring me joy, O Thou Who art the
most manifest of the manifest and the most
hidden of the hidden! —*Bahá'u'lláh*

He is the Gracious, the All-Bountiful!
O God, my God! Thy call hath attracted
me, and the voice of Thy Pen of Glory awakened me. The stream of Thy holy utterance
hath enraptured me, and the wine of Thine inspiration entranced me. Thou seest me, O Lord,
detached from all things but Thee, clinging to

the cord of Thy bounty and craving the wonders of Thy grace. I ask Thee, by the eternal billows of Thy loving-kindness and the shining lights of Thy tender care and favor, to grant that which shall draw me nigh unto Thee and make me rich in Thy wealth. My tongue, my pen, my whole being, testify to Thy power, Thy might, Thy grace and Thy bounty, that Thou art God and there is none other God but Thee, the Powerful, the Mighty.

I bear witness at this moment, O my God, to my helplessness and Thy sovereignty, my feebleness and Thy power. I know not that which profiteth me or harmeth me; Thou art, verily, the All-Knowing, the All-Wise. Do Thou decree for me, O Lord, my God, and my Master, that which will make me feel content with Thine eternal decree and will prosper me in every world of Thine. Thou art in truth the Gracious, the Bountiful.

Lord! Turn me not away from the ocean of Thy wealth and the heaven of Thy mercy, and ordain for me the good of this world and hereafter. Verily, Thou art the Lord of the mercy-seat, enthroned in the highest; there is none

other God but Thee, the One, the All-Knowing, the All-Wise. — *Bahá'u'lláh*

O my Lord! Make Thy beauty to be my
food, and Thy presence my drink, and
Thy pleasure my hope, and praise of Thee
my action, and remembrance of Thee my
companion, and the power of Thy sovereignty my succorer, and Thy habitation my
home, and my dwelling-place the seat Thou
hast sanctified from the limitations imposed
upon them who are shut out as by a veil from
Thee.

Thou art, verily, the Almighty, the All-Glorious, the Most Powerful. — *Bahá'u'lláh*

L auded be Thy Name, O Lord my God! I
am Thy servant who hath laid hold on
the cord of Thy tender mercies, and clung to
the hem of Thy bounteousness. I entreat
Thee by Thy name whereby Thou hast subjected all created things, both visible and invisible, and through which the breath that is
life indeed was wafted over the entire creation, to strengthen me by Thy power which

hath encompassed the heavens and the earth, and to guard me from all sickness and tribulation. I bear witness that Thou art the Lord of all names, and the Ordainer of all that may please Thee. There is none other God but Thee, the Almighty, the All-Knowing, the All-Wise.

Do Thou ordain for me, O my Lord, what will profit me in every world of Thy worlds. Supply me, then, with what Thou hast written down for the chosen ones among Thy creatures, whom neither the blame of the blamer, nor the clamor of the infidel, nor the estrangement of such as have withdrawn from Thee, hath deterred from turning towards Thee.

Thou, truly, art the Help in Peril through the power of Thy sovereignty. No God is there save Thee, the Almighty, the Most Powerful.

—*Bahá'u'lláh*

O my God, the God of bounty and mercy! Thou art that King by Whose commanding word the whole creation hath been called into being; and Thou art that All-Bountiful One the doings of Whose servants have never hindered Him from showing forth His grace, nor have they frustrated the revelations of His bounty.

Suffer this servant, I beseech Thee, to attain unto that which is the cause of his salvation in every world of Thy worlds. Thou art, verily, the Almighty, the Most Powerful, the All-Knowing, the All-Wise.   —*Bahá'u'lláh*

He is the prayer-hearing, prayer-answering God!

By Thy glory, O Beloved One, Thou giver of light to the world! The flames of separation have consumed me, and my waywardness hath melted my heart within me. I ask of Thee, by Thy Most Great Name, O Thou the Desire of the world and the Well-Beloved of mankind, to grant that the breeze of Thine inspiration may sustain my soul, that Thy wondrous voice may reach my ear, that my eyes may behold Thy signs and Thy light as revealed in the manifestations of Thy names and Thine attributes, O Thou within Whose grasp are all things!

Thou seest, O Lord my God, the tears of Thy favored ones, shed because of their sepa-

ration from Thee, and the fears of Thy devoted
ones in their remoteness from Thy Holy Court.
By Thy power that swayeth all things, visible
and invisible! It behooveth Thy loved ones to
shed tears of blood for that which hath befallen
the faithful at the hands of the wicked and the
oppressors on the earth. Thou beholdest, O my
God, how the ungodly have compassed Thy
cities and Thy realms! I ask Thee by Thy Messengers and Thy chosen ones and by Him
whereby the standard of Thy divine unity hath
been implanted amidst Thy servants, to shield
them by Thy bounty. Thou art, verily, the Gracious, the All-Bountiful.

And, again, I ask Thee by the sweet showers
of Thy grace and the billows of the ocean of
Thy favor, to ordain for Thy saints that which
shall solace their eyes and comfort their hearts.
Lord! Thou seest him that kneeleth yearning
to arise and serve Thee, the dead calling for
eternal life from the ocean of Thy favor and
craving to soar to the heavens of Thy wealth,
the stranger longing for his home of glory 'neath
the canopy of Thy grace, the seeker hastening
by Thy mercy to Thy door of bounty, the sin-

ful turning to the ocean of forgiveness and pardon.

By Thy sovereignty, O Thou Who art glorified in the hearts of men! I have turned to Thee, forsaking mine own will and desire, that Thy holy will and pleasure may rule within me and direct me according to that which the pen of Thy eternal decree hath destined for me. This servant, O Lord, though helpless turneth to the Orb of Thy Power, though abased hasteneth unto the Dayspring of Glory, though needy craveth the Ocean of Thy Grace. I beseech Thee by Thy favor and bounty, cast him not away.

Thou art verily the Almighty, the Pardoner, the Compassionate.   — *Bahá'u'lláh*

Glorified art Thou, O Lord my God! I give Thee thanks inasmuch as Thou hast called me into being in Thy days, and infused into me Thy love and Thy knowledge. I beseech Thee, by Thy name whereby the goodly pearls of Thy wisdom and Thine utterance were brought forth out of the treasuries of the hearts of such of Thy servants as are nigh unto Thee, and through which the Daystar of Thy name, the Compassionate, hath shed its radiance upon all that are in Thy heaven and on Thy earth, to supply me, by Thy grace and bounty, with Thy wondrous and hidden bounties.

These are the earliest days of my life, O my God, which Thou hast linked with Thine own days. Now that Thou hast conferred upon me so great an honor, withhold not from me the things Thou hast ordained for Thy chosen ones.

I am, O my God, but a tiny seed which Thou hast sown in the soil of Thy love, and caused to spring forth by the hand of Thy bounty. This seed craveth, therefore, in its inmost being, for the waters of Thy mercy and the living fountain of Thy grace. Send down upon it, from the heaven of Thy loving-kindness, that which will enable it to flourish beneath Thy shadow and within the borders of Thy court. Thou art He Who watereth the hearts of all that have recognized Thee from Thy plenteous stream and the fountain of Thy living waters.

Praised be God, the Lord of the worlds.

—*Bahá'u'lláh*

I beseech Thee, O my God, by all the transcendent glory of Thy Name, to clothe Thy loved ones in the robe of justice and to illumine their beings with the light of trustworthiness. Thou art the One that hath power to do as He pleaseth and Who holdeth within His grasp the reins of all things, visible and invisible.

— *Bahá'u'lláh*

Vouchsafe unto me, O my God, the full measure of Thy love and Thy good-pleasure, and through the attractions of Thy resplendent light enrapture our hearts, O Thou Who art the Supreme Evidence and the All-Glorified. Send down upon me, as a token of Thy grace, Thy vitalizing breezes, throughout the daytime and in the night season, O Lord of bounty.

No deed have I done, O my God, to merit beholding Thy face, and I know of a certainty that were I to live as long as the world lasts I would fail to accomplish any deed such as to deserve this favor, inasmuch as the station of a servant shall ever fall short of access to Thy holy precincts, unless Thy bounty should reach me and Thy tender mercy pervade me and Thy loving-kindness encompass me.

All praise be unto Thee, O Thou besides Whom there is none other God. Graciously enable me to ascend unto Thee, to be granted the honor of dwelling in Thy nearness and to have communion with Thee alone. No God is there but Thee.

Indeed shouldst Thou desire to confer blessing upon a servant Thou wouldst blot out from the realm of his heart every mention or disposition except Thine Own mention; and shouldst Thou ordain evil for a servant by reason of that which his hands have unjustly wrought before Thy face, Thou wouldst test him with the benefits of this world and of the next that he might become preoccupied therewith and forget Thy remembrance.

— *The Báb*

O my God! O my God! Glory be unto Thee for that Thou hast confirmed me to the confession of Thy oneness, attracted me unto the word of Thy singleness, enkindled me by the fire of Thy love, and occupied me with Thy mention and the service of Thy friends and maidservants.

O Lord, help me to be meek and lowly, and strengthen me in severing myself from all things and in holding to the hem of the garment of Thy glory, so that my heart may be filled with Thy love and leave no space for love of the world and attachment to its qualities.

O God! Sanctify me from all else save Thee, purge me from the dross of sins and transgressions, and cause me to possess a spiritual heart and conscience.

Verily, Thou art merciful and, verily, Thou art the Most Generous, Whose help is sought by all men.   — ʻAbduʼl-Bahá

O my Lord! O my Lord! This is a lamp lighted by the fire of Thy love and ablaze with the flame which is ignited in the tree of Thy mercy. O my Lord! Increase his enkindlement, heat and flame, with the fire which is kindled in the Sinai of Thy Manifestation. Verily, Thou art the Confirmer, the Assister, the Powerful, the Generous, the Loving.   — ʻAbduʼl-Bahá

O my God! O my God! This, Thy servant, hath advanced towards Thee, is
passionately wandering in the desert of Thy
love, walking in the path of Thy service, an-
ticipating Thy favors, hoping for Thy bounty, relying upon Thy kingdom, and intoxi-
cated by the wine of Thy gift. O my God!
Increase the fervor of his affection for Thee,
the constancy of his praise of Thee, and the
ardor of his love for Thee.

Verily, Thou art the Most Generous, the Lord
of grace abounding. There is no other God but
Thee, the Forgiving, the Merciful.

— *'Abdu'l-Bahá*

O God, my God! This is Thy radiant servant, Thy spiritual thrall, who hath
drawn nigh unto Thee and approached Thy
presence. He hath turned his face unto
Thine, acknowledging Thy oneness, confessing Thy singleness, and he hath called out in
Thy name among the nations, and led the
people to the streaming waters of Thy mercy,
O Thou most generous Lord! To those who
asked he hath given to drink from the cup of

guidance that brimmeth over with the wine of Thy measureless grace.

O Lord, assist him under all conditions, cause him to learn Thy well-guarded mysteries, and shower down upon him Thy hidden pearls. Make of him a banner rippling from castle summits in the winds of Thy heavenly aid, make of him a wellspring of crystal waters.

O my forgiving Lord! Light up the hearts with the rays of a lamp that sheddeth abroad its beams, disclosing to those among Thy people whom Thou hast bounteously favored, the realities of all things.

Verily, Thou art the Mighty, the Powerful, the Protector, the Strong, the Beneficent! Verily, Thou art the Lord of all mercies!

—'Abdu'l-Bahá

O God, my God! These are Thy feeble servants; they are Thy loyal bondsmen and Thy handmaidens, who have bowed themselves down before Thine exalted Utterance and humbled themselves at Thy Threshold of light, and borne witness to Thy oneness through which the Sun hath been made to shine in midday splendor. They have listened to the summons Thou didst raise from out Thy hidden Realm, and with hearts quivering with love and rapture, they have responded to Thy call.

O Lord, shower upon them all the outpourings of Thy mercy, rain down upon them all the waters of Thy grace. Make them to grow as beauteous plants in the garden of heaven, and from the full and brimming clouds of Thy bestowals and out of the deep pools of Thine abounding grace make Thou this garden to flower, and keep it ever green and lustrous, ever fresh and shimmering and fair.

Thou art, verily, the Mighty, the Exalted, the Powerful, He Who alone, in the heavens and on the earth, abideth unchanged. There is none other God save Thee, the Lord of manifest tokens and signs.   — 'Abdu'l-Bahá

He is God!
O God, my God! These are servants attracted in Thy days by the fragrances of Thy holiness, enkindled with the flame burning in

Thy holy tree, responding to Thy voice, uttering Thy praise, awakened by Thy breeze, stirred by Thy sweet savors, beholding Thy signs, understanding Thy verses, hearkening to Thy words, believing Thy Revelation and assured of Thy loving-kindness. Their eyes, O Lord, are fixed upon Thy kingdom of effulgent glory and their faces turned toward Thy dominion on high, their hearts beating with the love of Thy radiant and glorious beauty, their souls consumed with the flame of Thy love, O Lord of this world and the world hereafter, their lives seething with the ardor of their longing for Thee, and their tears poured forth for Thy sake.

Shield them within the stronghold of Thy protection and safety, preserve them in Thy watchful care, look upon them with the eyes of Thy providence and mercy, make them the signs of Thy divine unity that are manifest throughout all regions, the standards of Thy might that wave above Thy mansions of grandeur, the shining lamps that burn with the oil of Thy wisdom in the globes of Thy guidance, the birds of the garden of Thy knowledge that warble upon the topmost boughs in Thy sheltering paradise, and the leviathans of the ocean of Thy bounty that plunge by Thy supreme mercy in the fathomless deeps.

O Lord, my God! Lowly are these servants of Thine, exalt them in Thy kingdom on high; feeble, strengthen them by Thy supreme power; abased, bestow upon them Thy glory in Thine all-highest realm; poor, enrich them in Thy great dominion. Do Thou then ordain for them all the good Thou hast destined in Thy worlds, visible and invisible, prosper them in this world below, gladden their hearts with Thine inspiration, O Lord of all beings! Illumine their hearts with Thy joyful tidings diffused from Thine all-glorious Station, make firm their steps in Thy Most Great Covenant and strengthen their loins in Thy firm Testament, by Thy bounty and promised grace, O Gracious and Merciful One! Thou art, verily, the Gracious, the All-Bountiful.   —'Abdu'l-Bahá

O Thou Provider! Thou hast breathed over the friends in the West the sweet fragrance of the Holy Spirit, and with the light of divine guidance Thou hast lit up the western sky. Thou hast made those who were once remote to draw near unto Thyself; Thou hast turned strangers into loving friends; Thou hast awakened those who slept; Thou hast made the heedless mindful.

O Thou Provider! Assist Thou these noble friends to win Thy good pleasure, and make them well-wishers of stranger and friend alike. Bring them into the world that abideth forever; grant them a portion of heavenly grace; cause them to be true Bahá'ís, sincerely of God; save them from outward semblances, and establish them firmly in the truth. Make them signs and tokens of the Kingdom, luminous stars above the horizons of this nether life. Make them to be a comfort and a solace to humankind and servants to the peace of the world. Exhilarate them with the wine of Thy counsel, and grant that all of them may tread the path of Thy commandments.

O Thou Provider! The dearest wish of this servant of Thy Threshold is to behold the friends of East and West in close embrace; to see all the members of human society gathered with love in a single great assemblage, even as individual drops of water collected in one mighty sea; to behold them all as birds in one garden of roses, as pearls of one ocean, as leaves of one tree, as rays of one sun.

Thou art the Mighty, the Powerful, and Thou art the God of strength, the Omnipotent, the All-Seeing.   — 'Abdu'l-Bahá

STEADFASTNESS

I magnify Thy Name, O my God, and offer thanksgiving unto Thee, O my Desire, inasmuch as Thou hast enabled me to clearly perceive Thy straight Path, hast unveiled Thy Great Announcement before mine eyes and hast aided me to set my face towards the Dayspring of Thy Revelation and the Fountainhead of Thy Cause, whilst Thy servants and Thy people turned away from Thee. I entreat Thee, O Lord of the Kingdom of eternity, by the shrill voice of the Pen of Glory, and by the Burning Fire which calleth aloud from the verdant Tree, and by the Ark which Thou hast specially chosen for the people of Bahá, to grant that I may remain steadfast in my love for Thee, be well pleased with whatsoever Thou hast prescribed for me in Thy Book and may stand firm in Thy service and in the service of Thy loved ones.

Graciously assist then Thy servants, O my God, to do that which will serve to exalt Thy Cause and will enable them to observe whatsoever Thou hast revealed in Thy Book.

Verily Thou art the Lord of Strength, Thou art potent to ordain whatsoever Thou willest and within Thy grasp Thou holdest the reins of all created things. No God is there but Thee, the All-Powerful, the All-Knowing, the All-Wise.   —*Bahá'u'lláh*

Glorified be Thy name, O Lord my God! I beseech Thee by Thy power that hath encompassed all created things, and by Thy sovereignty that hath transcended the entire creation, and by Thy Word which was hidden in Thy wisdom and whereby Thou didst create Thy heaven and Thy earth, both to enable us to be steadfast in our love for Thee and in our obedience to Thy pleasure, and to fix our gaze upon Thy face, and celebrate Thy glory. Empower us, then, O my God, to spread abroad Thy signs among Thy creatures, and to guard Thy Faith in Thy realm. Thou hast ever existed independently of the mention of any of Thy creatures, and wilt remain as Thou hast been for ever and ever.

In Thee I have placed my whole confidence, unto Thee I have turned my face, to the cord of Thy loving providence I have clung, and towards the shadow of Thy mercy I have hastened. Cast me not as one disappointed out of Thy door, O my God, and withhold not from me Thy grace, for Thee alone do I seek. No God is there beside Thee, the Ever-Forgiving, the Most Bountiful.

Praise be to Thee, O Thou Who art the Beloved of them that have known Thee!

— *Bahá'u'lláh*

O Thou Whose nearness is my wish, Whose presence is my hope, Whose remembrance is my desire, Whose court of glory is my goal, Whose abode is my aim, Whose name is my healing, Whose love is the radiance of my heart, Whose service is my highest aspiration! I beseech Thee by Thy Name, through which Thou hast enabled them that have recognized Thee to soar to the sublimest heights of the knowledge of

Thee and empowered such as devoutly worship Thee to ascend into the precincts of the court of Thy holy favors, to aid me to turn my face towards Thy face, to fix mine eyes upon Thee, and to speak of Thy glory.

I am the one, O my Lord, who hath forgotten all else but Thee, and turned towards the Dayspring of Thy grace, who hath forsaken all save Thyself in the hope of drawing nigh unto Thy court. Behold me, then, with mine eyes lifted up towards the Seat that shineth with the splendors of the light of Thy Face. Send down, then, upon me, O my Beloved, that which will enable me to be steadfast in Thy Cause, so that the doubts of the infidels may not hinder me from turning towards Thee.

Thou art, verily, the God of Power, the Help in Peril, the All-Glorious, the Almighty.

—*Bahá'u'lláh*

O God, my God! I have turned in repentance unto Thee, and verily Thou art the Pardoner, the Compassionate.

O God, my God! I have returned to Thee, and verily Thou art the Ever-Forgiving, the Gracious.

O God, my God! I have clung to the cord of Thy bounty, and with Thee is the storehouse of all that is in heaven and earth.

O God, my God! I have hastened toward Thee, and verily Thou art the Forgiver, the Lord of grace abounding.

O God, my God! I thirst for the celestial wine of Thy grace, and verily Thou art the Giver, the Bountiful, the Gracious, the Almighty.

O God, my God! I testify that Thou hast revealed Thy Cause, fulfilled Thy promise and sent down from the heaven of Thy grace that which hath drawn unto Thee the hearts of Thy favored ones. Well is it with him that hath held fast unto Thy firm cord and clung to the hem of Thy resplendent robe!

I ask Thee, O Lord of all being and King of the seen and unseen, by Thy power, Thy majesty and Thy sovereignty, to grant that my name may be recorded by Thy pen of glory among Thy devoted ones, them whom the scrolls of the sinful hindered not from turning to the light of Thy countenance, O prayer-hearing, prayer-answering God!　　—*Bahá'u'lláh*

Glorified art Thou, O Lord my God! I beseech Thee by Him Who is Thy Most Great Name, Who hath been sorely afflicted by such of Thy creatures as have repudiated Thy truth, and Who hath been hemmed in by sorrows which no tongue can describe, to grant that I may remember Thee and celebrate Thy praise, in these days when all have turned away from Thy beauty, have disputed with Thee, and turned away disdainfully from Him Who is the Revealer of Thy Cause. None is there, O my Lord, to help Thee except Thine own Self, and no power to succor Thee save Thine own power.

I entreat Thee to enable me to cleave steadfastly to Thy love and Thy remembrance. This is, verily, within my power, and Thou art the One that knoweth all that is in me. Thou, in truth, art knowing, apprised of all. Deprive me not, O my Lord, of the splendors of the light of Thy face, whose brightness hath illuminated the whole world. No God is there beside Thee, the Most Powerful, the All-Glorious, the Ever-Forgiving.   —*Bahá'u'lláh*

Praise be to Thee, O Lord, my Best Beloved! Make me steadfast in Thy Cause, and grant that I may be reckoned among those who have not violated Thy Covenant nor followed the gods of their own idle fancy. Enable me, then, to obtain a seat of truth in Thy presence, bestow upon me a token of Thy mercy and let me join with such of Thy servants as shall have no fear nor shall they be put to grief. Abandon me not to myself, O my Lord, nor deprive me of recognizing Him Who is the Manifestation of Thine Own Self, nor account me with such as have turned away from Thy holy presence. Number me, O my God, with those who are privileged to fix their gaze upon Thy Beauty and who take such delight therein that they would not exchange a single moment thereof with the sovereignty of the kingdom of heavens and earth or with the entire realm of creation. Have mercy on me, O Lord, in these days when the peoples of Thine earth have erred grievously; supply me then, O my God, with that which is good and seemly in Thine estimation. Thou art, verily, the All-Powerful, the Gracious, the Bountiful, the Ever-Forgiving.

Grant, O my God, that I may not be reckoned among those whose ears are deaf, whose eyes are blind, whose tongues are speechless and whose hearts have failed to comprehend. Deliver me, O Lord, from the fire of ignorance and of selfish desire, suffer me to be admitted into the precincts of Thy transcendent mercy and send down upon me that which Thou hast ordained for Thy chosen ones. Potent art Thou to do what Thou willest. Verily, Thou art the Help in Peril, the Self-Subsisting. —*The Báb*

Praised and glorified art Thou, O God! Grant that the day of attaining Thy holy presence may be fast approaching. Cheer our hearts through the potency of Thy love and good-pleasure, and bestow upon us steadfastness that we may willingly submit to Thy Will and Thy Decree. Verily, Thy knowledge embraceth all the things Thou hast created or wilt create, and Thy celestial might transcendeth whatsoever Thou hast called or wilt call into being. There is none to be worshiped but Thee, there is none to be desired except Thee, there is none to be adored besides Thee and there is naught to be loved save Thy good-pleasure.

Verily, Thou art the supreme Ruler, the Sovereign Truth, the Help in Peril, the Self-Subsisting.   — *The Báb*

O Lord my God! Assist Thy loved ones to be firm in Thy Faith, to walk in Thy ways, to be steadfast in Thy Cause. Give them Thy grace to withstand the onslaught of self and passion, to follow the light of divine guidance. Thou art the Powerful, the Gracious, the Self-Subsisting, the Bestower, the Compassionate, the Almighty, the All-Bountiful.   — *'Abdu'l-Bahá*

O Thou, my God, Who guidest the seeker to the pathway that leadeth aright, Who deliverest the lost and blinded soul out of the wastes of perdition, Thou Who bestowest

upon the sincere great bounties and favors,
Who guardest the frightened within Thine
impregnable refuge, Who answerest, from
Thine all-highest horizon, the cry of those
who cry out unto Thee. Praised be Thou, O
my Lord! Thou hast guided the distracted
out of the death of unbelief, and hast
brought those who draw nigh unto Thee to
the journey's goal, and hast rejoiced the assured among Thy servants by granting them
their most cherished desires, and hast, from
Thy Kingdom of beauty, opened before the
faces of those who yearn after Thee the gates
of reunion, and hast rescued them from the
fires of deprivation and loss—so that they
hastened unto Thee and gained Thy presence, and arrived at Thy welcoming door,
and received of gifts an abundant share.

O my Lord, they thirsted, Thou didst lift to
their parched lips the waters of reunion. O Tender One, Bestowing One, Thou didst calm
their pain with the balm of Thy bounty and
grace, and didst heal their ailments with the
sovereign medicine of Thy compassion. O
Lord, make firm their feet on Thy straight path,

make wide for them the needle's eye, and cause them, dressed in royal robes, to walk in glory for ever and ever.

Verily, art Thou the Generous, the Ever-Giving, the Precious, the Most Bountiful. There is none other God but Thee, the Mighty, the Powerful, the Exalted, the Victorious.

— *'Abdu'l-Bahá*

TEACHING

GENERAL PRAYERS FOR TEACHING

Magnified be Thy name, O my God, for that Thou hast manifested the Day which is the King of Days, the Day which Thou didst announce unto Thy chosen Ones and Thy Prophets in Thy most excellent Tablets, the Day whereon Thou didst shed the splendor of the glory of all Thy names upon all created things. Great is his blessedness whosoever hath set himself towards Thee, and entered Thy presence, and caught the accents of Thy voice.

I beseech Thee, O my Lord, by the name of Him round Whom circleth in adoration the kingdom of Thy names, that Thou wilt graciously assist them that are dear to Thee to glorify Thy word among Thy servants, and to shed abroad Thy praise amidst Thy creatures, so that the ecstasies of Thy revelation may fill the souls of all the dwellers of Thine earth.

Since Thou hast guided them, O my Lord, unto the living waters of Thy grace, grant, by Thy bounty, that they may not be kept back from Thee; and since Thou hast summoned them to the habitation of Thy throne, drive them not out from Thy presence, through Thy loving-kindness. Send down upon them what shall wholly detach them from aught else except Thee, and make them able to soar in the atmosphere of Thy nearness, in such wise that neither the ascendancy of the oppressor nor the suggestions of them that have disbelieved in Thy most august and most mighty Self shall be capable of keeping them back from Thee.

—*Baháʼuʼlláh*

Praise be to Thee, O Lord my God! I implore Thee, by Thy Name which none hath befittingly recognized, and whose import no soul hath fathomed; I beseech Thee, by Him Who is the Fountainhead of Thy

Revelation and the Dayspring of Thy signs, to make my heart to be a receptacle of Thy love and of remembrance of Thee. Knit it, then, to Thy most great Ocean, that from it may flow out the living waters of Thy wisdom and the crystal streams of Thy glorification and praise.

The limbs of my body testify to Thy unity, and the hair of my head declareth the power of Thy sovereignty and might. I have stood at the door of Thy grace with utter self-effacement and complete abnegation, and clung to the hem of Thy bounty, and fixed mine eyes upon the horizon of Thy gifts.

Do Thou destine for me, O my God, what becometh the greatness of Thy majesty, and assist me, by Thy strengthening grace, so to teach Thy Cause that the dead may speed out of their sepulchers, and rush forth towards Thee, trusting wholly in Thee, and fixing their gaze upon the orient of Thy Cause, and the dawning-place of Thy Revelation.

Thou, verily, art the Most Powerful, the Most High, the All-Knowing, the All-Wise.

—*Bahá'u'lláh*

Glory be unto Thee, O Lord of the world and Desire of the nations, O Thou Who hast become manifest in the Greatest Name, whereby the pearls of wisdom and utterance have appeared from the shells of the great sea of Thy knowledge, and the heavens of divine revelation have been adorned with the light of the appearance of the sun of Thy countenance.

I beg of Thee, by that Word through which Thy proof was perfected among Thy creatures and Thy testimony was fulfilled amidst Thy servants, to strengthen Thy people in that whereby the face of the Cause will radiate in Thy dominion, the standards of Thy power will be planted among Thy servants, and the banners of Thy guidance will be raised throughout Thy dominions.

O my Lord! Thou beholdest them clinging to the rope of Thy grace and holding fast unto the hem of the mantle of Thy beneficence. Ordain for them that which may draw them nearer unto Thee, and withhold them from all else save Thee.

I beg of Thee, O Thou King of existence

and Protector of the seen and the unseen, to make whosoever arises to serve Thy Cause as a sea moving by Thy desire, as one ablaze with the fire of Thy Sacred Tree, shining from the horizon of the heaven of Thy will. Verily, Thou art the mighty One, Whom neither the power of all the world nor the strength of nations can weaken. There is no God but Thee, the One, the Incomparable, the Protector, the Self-Subsistent.   —*Bahá'u'lláh*

O God, Who art the Author of all Manifestations, the Source of all Sources, the Fountainhead of all Revelations, and the Wellspring of all Lights! I testify that by Thy Name the heaven of understanding hath been adorned, and the ocean of utterance hath surged, and the dispensations of Thy providence have been promulgated unto the followers of all religions.

I beseech Thee so to enrich me as to dispense with all save Thee, and be made independent of anyone except Thyself. Rain down, then, upon me out of the clouds of Thy bounty that which shall profit me in every world of Thy worlds. Assist me, then, through Thy strengthening grace, so to serve Thy Cause amidst Thy servants that I may show forth what will cause me to be remembered as long as Thine own kingdom endureth and Thy dominion will last.

This is Thy servant, O my Lord, who with his whole being hath turned unto the horizon of Thy bounty, and the ocean of Thy grace, and the heaven of Thy gifts. Do with me then as becometh Thy majesty, and Thy glory, and Thy bounteousness, and Thy grace.

Thou, in truth, art the God of strength and power, Who art meet to answer them that pray Thee. There is no God save Thee, the All-Knowing, the All-Wise. —*Bahá'u'lláh*

Say: Magnified be Thy Name, O Lord my God! I beseech Thee by Thy Name through which the splendor of the light of wisdom shone resplendent when the heavens of divine utterance were set in motion amidst mankind, to graciously aid me by Thy heavenly confirmations and enable me to extol Thy Name amongst Thy servants.

O Lord! Unto Thee have I turned my face,

detached from all save Thee and holding fast
to the hem of the robe of Thy manifold blessings. Unloose my tongue therefore to proclaim
that which will captivate the minds of men and
will rejoice their souls and spirits. Strengthen
me then in Thy Cause in such wise that I may
not be hindered by the ascendancy of the oppressors among Thy creatures nor withheld by
the onslaught of the disbelievers amidst those
who dwell in Thy realm. Make me as a lamp
shining throughout Thy lands that those in
whose hearts the light of Thy knowledge
gloweth and the yearning for Thy love lingereth
may be guided by its radiance.

Verily, potent art Thou to do whatsoever
Thou willest, and in Thy grasp Thou holdest
the kingdom of creation. There is none other
God but Thee, the Almighty, the All-Wise.

— Bahá'u'lláh

O my God, aid Thou Thy servant to raise
up the Word, and to refute what is vain
and false, to establish the truth, to spread the
sacred verses abroad, reveal the splendors,

and make the morning's light to dawn in the hearts of the righteous.

Thou art, verily, the Generous, the Forgiving. — *'Abdu'l-Bahá*

O God, my God! Aid Thou Thy trusted servants to have loving and tender hearts. Help them to spread, amongst all the nations of the earth, the light of guidance that cometh from the Company on high. Verily, Thou art the Strong, the Powerful, the Mighty, the All-Subduing, the Ever-Giving. Verily, Thou art the Generous, the Gentle, the Tender, the Most Bountiful.

— *'Abdu'l-Bahá*

Thou seest me, O my God, bowed down in lowliness, humbling myself before Thy commandments, submitting to Thy sovereignty, trembling at the might of Thy dominion, fleeing from Thy wrath, entreating Thy grace, relying upon Thy forgiveness, shaking with awe at Thy fury. I implore Thee with a throbbing heart, with streaming tears and a yearning soul, and in complete detachment from all things, to make Thy lovers as rays of light across Thy realms, and to aid Thy chosen servants to exalt Thy Word, that their faces may turn beauteous and bright with splendor, that their hearts may be filled with mysteries, and that every soul may lay down its burden of sin. Guard them then from the aggressor, from him who hath become a shameless and blasphemous doer of wrong.

Verily, Thy lovers thirst, O my Lord; lead them to the wellspring of bounty and grace. Verily, they hunger; send down unto them Thy heavenly table. Verily, they are naked; robe them in the garments of learning and knowledge.

Heroes are they, O my Lord, lead them to the field of battle. Guides are they, make them to speak out with arguments and proofs. Ministering servants are they, cause them to pass round the cup that brimmeth with the wine of certitude. O my God, make them to be songsters that carol in fair gardens, make them lions that couch in the thickets, whales that plunge in the vasty deep.

Verily, Thou art He of abounding grace. There is none other God save Thee, the Mighty, the Powerful, the Ever-Bestowing.

— *'Abdu'l-Bahá*

Thou knowest, O God, and art my witness that I have no desire in my heart save to attain Thy good pleasure, to be confirmed in servitude unto Thee, to consecrate myself in Thy service, to labor in Thy great vineyard and to sacrifice all in Thy path. Thou art the All-Knowing and the All-Seeing. I have no wish save to turn my steps, in my love for Thee, towards the mountains and the deserts to loudly proclaim the advent of Thy Kingdom, and to raise Thy call amidst all men. O God! Open Thou the way for this helpless one, grant Thou the remedy to this ailing one and bestow Thy healing upon this afflicted one. With burning heart and tearful eyes I supplicate Thee at Thy Threshold.

O God! I am prepared to endure any ordeal in Thy path and desire with all my heart and soul to meet any hardship.

O God! Protect me from tests. Thou knowest full well that I have turned away from all things and freed myself of all thoughts. I have no occupation save mention of Thee and no aspiration save serving Thee.   — 'Abdu'l-Bahá

PRAYERS FOR TEACHING
FROM THE TABLETS
OF THE DIVINE PLAN

REVEALED TO THE BAHÁ'ÍS OF THE
UNITED STATES AND CANADA

O Thou incomparable God! O Thou Lord of the Kingdom! These souls are Thy heavenly army. Assist them and, with the cohorts of the Supreme Concourse, make them victorious, so that each one of them may become like unto a regiment and conquer these countries through the love of God and the illumination of divine teachings.

O God! Be Thou their supporter and their helper, and in the wilderness, the mountain, the valley, the forests, the prairies and the seas, be Thou their confidant—so that they may cry out through the power of the Kingdom and the breath of the Holy Spirit.

Verily, Thou art the Powerful, the Mighty and the Omnipotent, and Thou art the Wise, the Hearing and the Seeing.   —*'Abdu'l-Bahá*

REVEALED TO THE BAHÁ'ÍS OF THE UNITED STATES AND CANADA

Whoever sets out on a teaching journey to any place, let him recite this prayer day and night during his travels in foreign lands.

O God, my God! Thou seest me enraptured and attracted toward Thy glorious kingdom, enkindled with the fire of Thy love amongst mankind, a herald of Thy kingdom in these vast and spacious lands, severed from aught else save Thee, relying on Thee, abandoning rest and comfort, remote from my native home, a wanderer in these regions, a stranger fallen upon the ground, humble before Thine exalted Threshold, submissive toward the heaven of Thine omnipotent glory, supplicating Thee in the dead of night and at the break of dawn, entreating and invoking Thee at morn and at eventide to graciously aid me to serve Thy Cause, to spread abroad Thy Teachings and to exalt Thy Word throughout the East and the West.

O Lord! Strengthen my back, enable me to serve Thee with the utmost endeavor, and leave me not to myself, lonely and helpless in these regions.

O Lord! Grant me communion with Thee in my loneliness, and be my companion in these foreign lands.

Verily, Thou art the Confirmer of whomsoever Thou willest in that which Thou desirest, and, verily, Thou art the All-Powerful, the Omnipotent.   — 'Abdu'l-Bahá

REVEALED TO THE BAHÁ'ÍS OF THE
UNITED STATES AND CANADA

Let whosoever travels to different parts to teach, peruse over mountain, desert, land and sea this supplication.

O God! O God! Thou seest my weakness, lowliness and humility before Thy creatures; nevertheless, I have trusted in Thee and have arisen in the promotion of Thy teachings among Thy strong servants, relying on Thy power and might.

O Lord! I am a broken-winged bird and desire to soar in Thy limitless space. How is it possible for me to do this save through Thy providence and grace, Thy confirmation and assistance.

O Lord! Have pity on my weakness, and strengthen me with Thy power. O Lord! Have pity on my impotence, and assist me with Thy might and majesty.

O Lord! Should the breath of the Holy Spirit confirm the weakest of creatures, he would attain all to which he aspireth and would possess anything he desireth. Indeed, Thou hast assisted Thy servants in the past and, though they were the weakest of Thy creatures, the lowliest of Thy servants and the most insignificant of those who lived upon the earth, through Thy sanction and potency they took precedence over the most glorious of Thy people and the most noble of mankind. Whereas formerly they were as moths, they became as royal falcons, and whereas before they were as brooks, they became as seas, through Thy bestowal and Thy mercy. They became, through Thy most great favor, stars shining on the horizon of guidance, birds singing in the rose gardens of immortality, lions roaring in the forests of knowledge and wisdom, and whales swimming in the oceans of life.

Verily, Thou art the Clement, the Powerful, the Mighty, and the Most Merciful of the merciful.

—'Abdu'l-Bahá

REVEALED TO THE BAHÁ'ÍS OF THE UNITED STATES AND CANADA

O God, my God! Thou seest how black darkness is enshrouding all regions, how all countries are burning with the flame of dissension, and the fire of war and carnage is blazing throughout the East and the West. Blood is flowing, corpses bestrew the ground, and severed heads are fallen on the dust of the battlefield.

O Lord! Have pity on these ignorant ones, and look upon them with the eye of forgiveness and pardon. Extinguish this fire, so that these dense clouds which obscure the horizon may be scattered, the Sun of Reality shine forth with the rays of conciliation, this intense gloom be dispelled and the resplendent light of peace shed its radiance upon all countries.

O Lord! Draw up the people from the abyss of the ocean of hatred and enmity, and deliver them from this impenetrable darkness. Unite their hearts, and brighten their eyes with the light of peace and reconciliation. Deliver them from the depths of war and bloodshed, and free them from the darkness of error. Remove the veil from their eyes, and enlighten their hearts with the light of guidance. Treat them with Thy tender mercy and compassion, and deal not with them according to Thy justice and wrath which cause the limbs of the mighty to quake.

O Lord! Wars have persisted. Distress and anxiety have waxed great, and every flourishing region is laid waste.

O Lord! Hearts are heavy, and souls are in anguish. Have mercy on these poor souls, and do not leave them to the excesses of their own desires.

O Lord! Make manifest in Thy lands humble and submissive souls, their faces illumined with the rays of guidance, severed from the world, extolling Thy Name, uttering Thy praise, and diffusing the fragrance of Thy holiness amongst mankind.

O Lord! Strengthen their backs, gird up their loins, and enrapture their hearts with the most mighty signs of Thy love.

O Lord! Verily, they are weak, and Thou art the Powerful and the Mighty; they are impotent, and Thou art the Helper and the Merciful.

O Lord! The ocean of rebellion is surging, and these tempests will not be stilled save through Thy boundless grace which hath embraced all regions.

O Lord! Verily, the people are in the abyss of passion, and naught can save them but Thine infinite bounties.

O Lord! Dispel the darkness of these corrupt desires, and illumine the hearts with the lamp of Thy love through which all countries will erelong be enlightened. Confirm, moreover, Thy loved ones, those who, leaving their homelands, their families and their children, have, for the love of Thy Beauty, traveled to foreign countries to diffuse Thy fragrances and promulgate Thy Teachings. Be Thou their companion in their loneliness, their helper in a strange land, the remover of their sorrows, their comforter in calamity. Be Thou a refreshing draught for their thirst, a healing medicine for their ills and a balm for the burning ardor of their hearts.

Verily, Thou art the Most Generous, the Lord of grace abounding, and, verily, Thou art the Compassionate and the Merciful.

—*'Abdu'l-Bahá*

REVEALED TO THE BAHÁ'ÍS OF THE NORTHEASTERN STATES

The following supplication is to be read by the teachers and friends daily:

O Thou kind Lord! Praise be unto Thee that Thou hast shown us the highway of guidance, opened the doors of the kingdom and manifested Thyself through the Sun of

Reality. To the blind Thou hast given sight; to the deaf Thou hast granted hearing; Thou hast resuscitated the dead; Thou hast enriched the poor; Thou hast shown the way to those who have gone astray; Thou hast led those with parched lips to the fountain of guidance; Thou hast suffered the thirsty fish to reach the ocean of reality; and Thou hast invited the wandering birds to the rose garden of grace.

O Thou Almighty! We are Thy servants and Thy poor ones; we are remote and yearn for Thy presence, are athirst for the water of Thy fountain, are ill, longing for Thy healing. We are walking in Thy path and have no aim or hope save the diffusion of Thy fragrance, so that all souls may raise the cry of "O God, guide us to the straight path." May their eyes be opened to behold the light, and may they be freed from the darkness of ignorance. May they gather around the lamp of Thy guidance. May every portionless one receive a share. May the deprived become the confidants of Thy mysteries.

O Almighty! Look upon us with the glance

of mercifulness. Grant us heavenly confirmation. Bestow upon us the breath of the Holy Spirit, so that we may be assisted in Thy service and, like unto brilliant stars, shine in these regions with the light of Thy guidance.

Verily, Thou art the Powerful, the Mighty, the Wise and the Seeing.   —*'Abdu'l-Bahá*

REVEALED TO THE BAHÁ'ÍS OF THE SOUTHERN STATES

Every soul who travels through the cities, villages and hamlets of these States and is engaged in the diffusion of the fragrances of God, should peruse this commune every morning:

O my God! O my God! Thou seest me in my lowliness and weakness, occupied with the greatest undertaking, determined to raise Thy word among the masses and to spread Thy teachings among Thy peoples. How can I succeed unless Thou assist me with the breath of the Holy Spirit, help me to triumph by the hosts of Thy glorious kingdom, and shower upon me Thy confirmations, which alone can change a gnat into an eagle, a drop of water into rivers and seas, and an atom into lights and suns? O my Lord! Assist me with Thy triumphant and effective might, so that my tongue may utter Thy praises and attributes among all people and my soul overflow with the wine of Thy love and knowledge.

Thou art the Omnipotent and the Doer of whatsoever Thou willest. —'Abdu'l-Bahá

REVEALED TO THE BAHÁ'ÍS OF THE CENTRAL STATES

Let the spreaders of the fragrances of God recite this prayer every morning:

O Lord, my God! Praise and thanksgiving be unto Thee for Thou hast guided me to the highway of the kingdom, suffered me to walk in this straight and far-stretching path, illumined my eye by beholding the splendors of Thy light, inclined my ear to the melodies of the birds of holiness from the kingdom of mysteries and attracted my heart with Thy love among the righteous.

O Lord! Confirm me with the Holy Spirit, so that I may call in Thy Name amongst the nations and give the glad tidings of the mani-festation of Thy kingdom amongst mankind.

O Lord! I am weak, strengthen me with Thy power and potency. My tongue falters, suffer me to utter Thy commemoration and praise. I am lowly, honor me through admitting me into Thy kingdom. I am remote, cause me to ap-proach the threshold of Thy mercifulness. O Lord! Make me a brilliant lamp, a shining star and a blessed tree, adorned with fruit, its branches overshadowing all these regions. Ver-ily, Thou art the Mighty, the Powerful and Unconstrained.   —'Abdu'l-Bahá

REVEALED TO THE BAHÁ'ÍS OF THE
WESTERN STATES

The following commune is to be read . . . every day:

O God! O God! This is a broken-winged bird and his flight is very slow—assist him so that he may fly toward the apex of prosperity and salvation, wing his way with the utmost joy and happiness throughout the illimitable space, raise his melody in Thy Supreme Name in all the regions, exhilarate the ears with this call, and brighten the eyes by beholding the signs of guidance.

O Lord! I am single, alone and lowly. For me there is no support save Thee, no helper except Thee and no sustainer beside Thee. Confirm me in Thy service, assist me with the cohorts of Thy angels, make me victorious in the promotion of Thy Word and suffer me to speak out Thy wisdom amongst Thy creatures. Verily, Thou art the helper of the weak and the defender of the little ones, and verily Thou art the Powerful, the Mighty and the Unconstrained.

— 'Abdu'l-Bahá

REVEALED TO THE BAHÁ'ÍS OF CANADA

Praise be to Thee, O my God! These are Thy servants who are attracted by the fragrances of Thy mercifulness, are enkindled by the fire burning in the tree of Thy singleness, and whose eyes are brightened by beholding the splendors of the light shining in the Sinai of Thy oneness.

O Lord! Loose their tongues to make mention of Thee amongst Thy people, suffer them to speak forth Thy praise through Thy grace and loving-kindness, assist them with the cohorts of Thine angels, strengthen their loins in Thy service, and make them the signs of Thy guidance amongst Thy creatures.

Verily, Thou art the All-Powerful, the Most Exalted, the Ever-Forgiving, the All-Merciful.

—'Abdu'l-Bahá

REVEALED TO THE BAHÁ'ÍS OF CANADA

The spreaders of the fragrances of God should recite this prayer every morning:

O God, my God! Thou beholdest this weak one begging for celestial strength, this poor one craving Thy heavenly treasures, this thirsty one longing for the fountain of eternal life, this afflicted one yearning for Thy promised healing through Thy boundless mercy which Thou hast destined for Thy chosen servants in Thy kingdom on high.

O Lord! I have no helper save Thee, no shelter besides Thee, and no sustainer except Thee. Assist me with Thine angels to diffuse Thy holy fragrances and to spread abroad Thy teachings amongst the choicest of Thy people.

O my Lord! Suffer me to be detached from aught else save Thee, to hold fast to the hem of Thy bounty, to be wholly devoted to Thy Faith, to remain fast and firm in Thy love and to observe what Thou hast prescribed in Thy Book.

Verily, Thou art the Powerful, the Mighty, the Omnipotent.   —'Abdu'l-Bahá

TESTS AND DIFFICULTIES

O Thou Whose tests are a healing medicine to such as are nigh unto Thee, Whose sword is the ardent desire of all them that love Thee, Whose dart is the dearest wish of those hearts that yearn after Thee, Whose decree is the sole hope of them that have recognized Thy truth! I implore Thee, by Thy divine sweetness and by the splendors of the glory of Thy face, to send down upon us from Thy retreats on high that which will enable us to draw nigh unto Thee. Set, then, our feet firm, O my God, in Thy Cause, and enlighten our hearts with the effulgence of Thy knowledge, and illumine our breasts with the brightness of Thy names.

—*Bahá'u'lláh*

Glory to Thee, O my God! But for the tribulations which are sustained in Thy path, how could Thy true lovers be recognized; and were it not for the trials which are borne for love of Thee, how could the station of such as yearn for Thee be revealed? Thy might beareth me witness! The companions of all who adore Thee are the tears they shed, and the comforters of such as seek Thee are the groans they utter, and the food of them who haste to meet Thee is the fragments of their broken hearts.

How sweet to my taste is the bitterness of death suffered in Thy path, and how precious in my estimation are the shafts of Thine enemies when encountered for the sake of the exaltation of Thy word! Let me quaff in Thy Cause, O my God, whatsoever Thou didst desire, and send down upon me in Thy love all Thou didst ordain. By Thy glory! I wish only what Thou wishest, and cherish what Thou cherishest. In Thee have I, at all times, placed my whole trust and confidence.

Raise up, I implore Thee, O my God, as helpers to this Revelation such as shall be counted worthy of Thy name and of Thy sovereignty, that they may remember me among

Thy creatures, and hoist the ensigns of Thy victory in Thy land.

Potent art Thou to do what pleaseth Thee. No God is there but Thee, the Help in Peril, the Self-Subsisting. —*Bahá'u'lláh*

Glorified art Thou, O Lord my God! Every man of insight confesseth Thy sovereignty and Thy dominion, and every discerning eye perceiveth the greatness of Thy majesty and the compelling power of Thy might. The winds of tests are powerless to hold back them that enjoy near access to Thee from setting their faces towards the horizon of Thy glory, and the tempests of trials must fail to draw away and hinder such as are wholly devoted to Thy will from approaching Thy court.

Methinks, the lamp of Thy love is burning in their hearts, and the light of Thy tenderness is lit within their breasts. Adversities are incapable of estranging them from Thy Cause, and the vicissitudes of fortune can never cause them to stray from Thy pleasure.

I beseech Thee, O my God, by them and by

the sighs which their hearts utter in their separation from Thee, to keep them safe from the mischief of Thine adversaries, and to nourish their souls with what Thou hast ordained for Thy loved ones on whom shall come no fear and who shall not be put to grief.

—*Bahá'u'lláh*

Dispel my grief by Thy bounty and Thy generosity, O God, my God, and banish mine anguish through Thy sovereignty and Thy might. Thou seest me, O my God, with my face set towards Thee at a time when sorrows have compassed me on every side. I implore Thee, O Thou Who art the Lord of all being, and overshadowest all things visible and invisible, by Thy Name whereby Thou hast subdued the hearts and the souls of men, and by the billows of the Ocean of Thy mercy and the splendors of the Daystar of Thy bounty, to number me with them whom nothing whatsoever hath deterred from setting their faces toward Thee, O Thou Lord of all names and Maker of the heavens!

Thou beholdest, O my Lord, the things

which have befallen me in Thy days. I entreat
Thee, by Him Who is the Dayspring of Thy
names and the Dawning-Place of Thine attributes, to ordain for me what will enable me
to arise to serve Thee and to extol Thy virtues.
Thou art, verily, the Almighty, the Most Powerful, Who art wont to answer the prayers of
all men!

And, finally, I beg of Thee by the light of
Thy countenance to bless my affairs, and re-
deem my debts, and satisfy my needs. Thou
art He to Whose power and to Whose dominion every tongue hath testified, and Whose
majesty and Whose sovereignty every understanding heart hath acknowledged. No God is
there but Thee, Who hearest and art ready to
answer.   —*Bahá'u'lláh*

Lauded and glorified art Thou, O my God!
I entreat Thee by the sighing of Thy lovers and by the tears shed by them that long to
behold Thee, not to withhold from me Thy
tender mercies in Thy Day, nor to deprive me

of the melodies of the Dove that extolleth
Thy oneness before the light that shineth
from Thy face. I am the one who is in misery,
O God! Behold me cleaving fast to Thy
Name, the All-Possessing. I am the one who
is sure to perish; behold me clinging to Thy
Name, the Imperishable. I implore Thee,
therefore, by Thy Self, the Exalted, the Most
High, not to abandon me unto mine own self
and unto the desires of a corrupt inclination.
Hold Thou my hand with the hand of Thy
power, and deliver me from the depths of my
fancies and idle imaginings, and cleanse me
of all that is abhorrent unto Thee.

Cause me, then, to turn wholly unto Thee,
to put my whole trust in Thee, to seek Thee as
my Refuge, and to flee unto Thy face. Thou
art, verily, He Who, through the power of His
might, doeth whatsoever He desireth, and
commandeth, through the potency of His will,
whatsoever He chooseth. None can withstand
the operation of Thy decree; none can divert
the course of Thine appointment. Thou art,
in truth, the Almighty, the All-Glorious, the
Most Bountiful.   —*Bahá'u'lláh*

Is there any Remover of difficulties save God? Say: Praised be God! He is God! All are His servants, and all abide by His bidding!
                   — *The Báb*

Thou knowest full well, O my God, that tribulations have showered upon me from all directions and that no one can dispel or transmute them except Thee. I know of a certainty, by virtue of my love for Thee, that Thou wilt never cause tribulations to befall any soul unless Thou desirest to exalt his station in Thy celestial Paradise and to buttress his heart in this earthly life with the bulwark of Thine all-compelling power, that it may not become inclined toward the vanities of this world. Indeed Thou art well aware that under all conditions I would cherish the remembrance of Thee far more than the ownership of all that is in the heavens and on the earth.

Strengthen my heart, O my God, in Thine obedience and in Thy love, and grant that I may be clear of the entire company of Thine adversaries. Verily, I swear by Thy glory that I yearn for naught besides Thyself, nor do I desire anything except Thy mercy, nor am I apprehensive of aught save Thy justice. I beg Thee to forgive me as well as those whom Thou lovest, howsoever Thou pleasest. Verily, Thou art the Almighty, the Bountiful.

Immensely exalted art Thou, O Lord of the heavens and earth, above the praise of all men, and may peace be upon Thy faithful servants and glory be unto God, the Lord of all the worlds. — *The Báb*

I adjure Thee by Thy might, O my God! Let no harm beset me in times of tests, and in moments of heedlessness guide my steps aright through Thine inspiration. Thou art God, potent art Thou to do what Thou desirest. No one can withstand Thy Will or thwart Thy Purpose. — *The Báb*

O Lord! Thou art the Remover of every anguish and the Dispeller of every affliction. Thou art He Who banisheth every sorrow and setteth free every slave, the Redeemer of every soul. O Lord! Grant deliverance through Thy mercy, and reckon me among such servants of Thine as have gained salvation.   — *The Báb*

TRIUMPH OF THE CAUSE

Thou seest, O my God, how Thy loved ones have been encompassed by the rebellious amongst Thy creatures and the wicked amidst Thy people. No land remaineth but the lamentation of Thy lovers and the wailing of Thy chosen ones were lifted up therein. I beseech Thee by Thy Most Great Name to draw forth the hand of power from the bosom of Thy might and to assist therewith all them that love Thee.

Thou beholdest, O my God, their eyes turned towards Thee, their gaze fixed upon the Dayspring of Thy might and Thy loving providence. Transmute, O my Lord, their abasement into glory, their poverty into wealth, and their weakness into a strength born of Thee.

Powerful art Thou to do whatsoever Thou willest. No God is there but Thee, the All-Knowing, the All-Informed. *—Bahá'u'lláh*

Glory be to Thee, O Lord my God! Make manifest the rivers of Thy sovereign might, that the waters of Thy Unity may flow through the inmost realities of all things, in such wise that the banner of Thine unfailing guidance may be raised aloft in the kingdom of Thy command and the stars of Thy divine splendor may shine brightly in the heaven of Thy majesty.

Potent art Thou to do what pleaseth Thee. Thou, verily, art the Help in Peril, the Self-Subsisting.   —*Bahá'u'lláh*

Suffer me not, O God, my God, to be kept back from the heaven of Thy bounties and the daystar of Thy favors. I beseech Thee by that Word through which Thou hast subdued all things visible and invisible to assist me and to assist Thy chosen ones to accomplish that which shall exalt Thy Cause amidst Thy servants and throughout Thy regions. Do Thou ordain for me, then, every good thing which Thou hast sent down in Thy Book.

Verily Thou art the Almighty, the Ever-Forgiving, the Most Generous.   —*Bahá'u'lláh*

Glory be unto Thee, O Lord, Thou Who hast brought into being all created things, through the power of Thy behest.

O Lord! Assist those who have renounced all else but Thee, and grant them a mighty victory. Send down upon them, O Lord, the concourse of the angels in heaven and earth and all that is between, to aid Thy servants, to succor and strengthen them, to enable them to achieve success, to sustain them, to invest them with glory, to confer upon them honor and exaltation, to enrich them and to make them triumphant with a wondrous triumph.

Thou art their Lord, the Lord of the heavens and the earth, the Lord of all the worlds. Strengthen this Faith, O Lord, through the power of these servants, and cause them to prevail over all the peoples of the world; for they, of a truth, are Thy servants who have detached themselves from aught else but Thee, and Thou, verily, art the protector of true believers.

Grant Thou, O Lord, that their hearts may, through allegiance to this, Thine inviolable Faith, grow stronger than anything else in the heavens and on earth and in whatsoever is between them; and strengthen, O Lord, their hands with the tokens of Thy wondrous power that they may manifest Thy power before the gaze of all mankind.   *— The Báb*

O Lord! Provide for the speedy growth of the Tree of Thy divine Unity; water it then, O Lord, with the flowing waters of Thy good-pleasure, and cause it, before the revelations of Thy divine assurance, to yield such fruits as Thou desirest for Thy glorification and exaltation, Thy praise and thanksgiving, and to magnify Thy Name, to laud the oneness of Thine Essence and to offer adoration unto Thee, inasmuch as all this lieth within Thy grasp and in that of none other.

Great is the blessedness of those whose blood Thou hast chosen wherewith to water the Tree of Thine affirmation, and thus to exalt Thy holy and immutable Word.   *— The Báb*

O Lord! Render victorious Thy forbearing servants in Thy days by granting them a befitting victory, inasmuch as they have sought martyrdom in Thy path. Send down upon them that which will bring comfort to their minds, will rejoice their inner beings, will impart assurance to their hearts and tranquillity to their bodies and will enable their souls to ascend to the presence of God, the Most Exalted, and to attain the supreme Paradise and such retreats of glory as Thou hast destined for men of true knowledge and virtue. Verily, Thou knowest all things, while we are but Thy servants, Thy thralls, Thy bondsmen and Thy poor ones. No Lord but Thee do we invoke, O God our Lord, nor do we implore blessings or grace from anyone but Thee, O Thou Who art the God of mercy unto this world and the next. We are but the embodiments of poverty, of nothingness, of helplessness and of perdition, while Thy whole Being betokeneth wealth, independence, glory, majesty and boundless grace.

Turn our recompense, O Lord, into that

which well beseemeth Thee of the good of this world and of the next, and of the manifold bounties which extend from on high down to the earth below.

Verily, Thou art our Lord and the Lord of all things. Into Thy hands do we surrender ourselves, yearning for the things that pertain unto Thee. — *The Báb*

O Lord! Enable all the peoples of the earth to gain admittance into the Paradise of Thy Faith, so that no created being may remain beyond the bounds of Thy goodpleasure.

From time immemorial Thou hast been potent to do what pleaseth Thee and transcendent above whatsoever Thou desirest.

— *The Báb*

O God, my God! Praise be unto Thee for kindling the fire of divine love in the Holy Tree on the summit of the loftiest mount: that Tree which is "neither of the

East nor of the West,"* that fire which blazed out till the flame of it soared upward to the Concourse on high, and from it those realities caught the light of guidance, and cried out: "Verily have we perceived a fire on the slope of Mount Sinai."†

O God, my God! Increase Thou this fire, as day followeth day, till the blast of it setteth in motion all the earth. O Thou, my Lord! Kindle the light of Thy love in every heart, breathe into men's souls the spirit of Thy knowledge, gladden their breasts with the verses of Thy oneness. Call Thou to life those who dwell in their tombs, warn Thou the prideful, make happiness worldwide, send down Thy crystal waters, and in the assemblage of manifest splendors, pass round that cup which is "tempered at the camphor fountain."‡

Verily, art Thou the Giving, the Forgiving, the Ever-Bestowing. Verily, art Thou the Merciful, the Compassionate. —'Abdu'l-Bahá

* Qur'án 24:35.
† cf. Qur'án 28:29.
‡Qur'án 76:5.

He is God!

O Lord, my God, my Well-Beloved! These are servants of Thine that have heard Thy Voice, given ear to Thy Word and hearkened to Thy Call. They have believed in Thee, witnessed Thy wonders, acknowledged Thy proof and testified to Thine evidence. They have walked in Thy ways, followed Thy guidance, discovered Thy mysteries, comprehended the secrets of Thy Book, the verses of Thy Scrolls and the tidings of Thy Epistles and Tablets. They have clung to the hem of Thy garment and held fast unto the robe of Thy light and grandeur. Their footsteps have been strengthened in Thy Covenant and their hearts made firm in Thy Testament. Lord! Do Thou kindle in their hearts the flame of Thy divine attraction and grant that the bird of love and understanding may sing within their hearts. Grant that they may be even as potent signs, resplendent standards, and perfect as Thy Word. Exalt by them Thy Cause, unfurl Thy banners and publish far and wide Thy wonders. Make by them Thy Word triumphant, and strengthen the loins of Thy loved ones. Unloose their tongues to laud Thy Name, and inspire them to do Thy holy will and pleasure. Illumine their faces in Thy Kingdom of holiness, and perfect their joy by aiding them to arise for the triumph of Thy Cause.

Lord! Feeble are we, strengthen us to diffuse the fragrances of Thy Holiness; poor, enrich us from the treasures of Thy Divine Unity; naked, clothe us with the robe of Thy bounty; sinful, forgive us our sins by Thy grace, Thy favor and Thy pardon. Thou art, verily, the Aider, the Helper, the Gracious, the Mighty, the Powerful.

The glory of glories rest upon them that are fast and firm.   —'Abdu'l-Bahá

UNITY

O my God! O my God! Unite the hearts of Thy servants, and reveal to them Thy great purpose. May they follow Thy commandments and abide in Thy law. Help them, O God, in their endeavor, and grant them strength to serve Thee. O God! Leave them not to themselves, but guide their steps by the light of Thy knowledge, and cheer their hearts by Thy love. Verily, Thou art their Helper and their Lord. —*Bahá'u'lláh*

O my God! O my God! Verily, I invoke Thee and supplicate before Thy threshold, asking Thee that all Thy mercies may descend upon these souls. Specialize them for Thy favor and Thy truth.

O Lord! Unite and bind together the hearts, join in accord all the souls, and exhilarate the spirits through the signs of Thy sanctity and oneness. O Lord! Make these faces radiant through the light of Thy oneness. Strengthen the loins of Thy servants in the service of Thy kingdom.

O Lord, Thou possessor of infinite mercy! O Lord of forgiveness and pardon! Forgive our sins, pardon our shortcomings, and cause us to turn to the kingdom of Thy clemency, invoking the kingdom of might and power, humble at Thy shrine and submissive before the glory of Thine evidences.

O Lord God! Make us as waves of the sea, as flowers of the garden, united, agreed through the bounties of Thy love. O Lord! Dilate the breasts through the signs of Thy oneness, and make all mankind as stars shining from the same height of glory, as perfect fruits growing upon Thy tree of life.

Verily, Thou art the Almighty, the Self-Subsistent, the Giver, the Forgiving, the Pardoner, the Omniscient, the One Creator.

—*'Abdu'l-Bahá*

WOMEN

O Thou Whose face is the object of the adoration of all that yearn after Thee, Whose presence is the hope of such as are wholly devoted to Thy will, Whose nearness is the desire of all that have drawn nigh unto Thy court, Whose countenance is the companion of those who have recognized Thy truth, Whose name is the mover of the souls that long to behold Thy face, Whose voice is the true life of Thy lovers, the words of Whose mouth are as the waters of life unto all who are in heaven and on earth!

I beseech Thee, by the wrong Thou hast suffered and the ills inflicted upon Thee by the hosts of wrongful doers, to send down upon me from the clouds of Thy mercy that which will purify me of all that is not of Thee, that I may be worthy to praise Thee and fit to love Thee.

Withhold not from me, O my Lord, the things Thou didst ordain for such of Thy handmaidens as circle around Thee, and on whom are poured continually the splendors of the sun of Thy beauty and the beams of the brightness of Thy face. Thou art He Who from everlasting hath succored whosoever hath sought Thee, and bountifully favored him who hath asked Thee.

No God is there beside Thee, the Mighty, the Ever-Abiding, the All-Bounteous, the Most Generous.   —*Bahá'u'lláh*

Glory be to Thee, O my God! My face hath been set towards Thy face, and my face is, verily, Thy face, and my call is Thy call, and my Revelation Thy Revelation, and my self Thy Self, and my Cause Thy Cause, and my behest Thy behest, and my Being Thy Being, and my sovereignty Thy sovereignty, and my glory Thy glory, and my power Thy power.

I implore Thee, O Thou Fashioner of the nations and the King of eternity, to guard Thy handmaidens within the tabernacle of Thy chastity, and to cancel such of their deeds as are unworthy of Thy days. Purge out, then, from them, O my God, all doubts and idle fancies, and sanctify them from whatsoever becometh not their kinship with Thee, O Thou Who art the Lord of names, and the Source of utterance. Thou art He in Whose grasp are the reins of the entire creation.

No God is there but Thee, the Almighty, the Most Exalted, the All-Glorious, the Self-Subsisting.   —*Bahá'u'lláh*

Glorified art Thou, O Lord my God! Thou art He the fire of Whose love hath set ablaze the hearts of them who have recognized Thy unity, and the splendors of Whose countenance have illuminated the faces of such as have drawn nigh unto Thy court. How plenteous, O my God, is the stream of Thy knowledge! How sweet, O my Beloved, is the injury which, in my love for Thee, and for the sake of Thy pleasure, I suffer from the darts of the wicked doers! How pleasing are the wounds which, in Thy path and in order to proclaim Thy Faith, I sustain from the swords of the infidels!

I beseech Thee, by Thy name through which Thou turnest restlessness into tranquillity, fear into confidence, weakness into strength, and abasement into glory, that Thou of Thy grace wilt aid me and Thy servants to exalt Thy name, to deliver Thy Message, and to proclaim Thy Cause, in such wise that we may remain unmoved by either the assaults of the transgressors or the wrath of the infidels, O Thou Who art my Well-Beloved!

I am, O my Lord, Thy handmaiden, who hath hearkened to Thy call, and hastened unto Thee, fleeing from herself and resting her heart upon Thee. I implore Thee, O my Lord, by Thy name out of which all the treasures of the earth were brought forth, to shield me from the hints of such as have disbelieved in Thee and repudiated Thy truth.

Powerful art Thou to do what Thou pleasest. Thou art, verily, the All-Knowing, the All-Wise. —*Bahá'u'lláh*

Magnified be Thy name, O Lord my God! Behold Thou mine eye expectant to gaze on the wonders of Thy mercy, and mine ear longing to hearken unto Thy sweet melodies, and my heart yearning for the living waters of Thy knowledge. Thou seest Thy handmaiden, O my God, standing before the habitation of Thy mercy, and calling upon Thee by Thy name which Thou hast chosen above all other names and set up over all that are in heaven and on earth. Send down upon her the breaths of Thy mercy, that she may be carried away wholly from herself, and be drawn entirely towards the seat which, resplendent with the glory of Thy face, sheddeth afar the radiance of Thy sovereignty, and is established as Thy throne. Potent art Thou to do what Thou willest. No God is there beside Thee, the All-Glorious, the Most Bountiful.

Cast not out, I entreat Thee, O my Lord, them that have sought Thee, and turn not away such as have directed their steps towards Thee, and deprive not of Thy grace all that love Thee. Thou art He, O my Lord, Who hath called

Himself the God of Mercy, the Most Compassionate. Have mercy, then, upon Thy handmaiden who hath sought Thy shelter, and set her face towards Thee.

Thou art, verily, the Ever-Forgiving, the Most Merciful.   —*Bahá'u'lláh*

O Thou, at Whose dreadful majesty all things have trembled, in Whose grasp are the affairs of all men, towards Whose grace and mercy are set the faces of all Thy creatures! I entreat Thee, by Thy Name which Thou hast ordained to be the spirit of all names that are in the kingdom of names, to shield us from the whisperings of those who have turned away from Thee, and have repudiated the truth of Thy most august and most exalted Self, in this Revelation that hath caused the kingdom of Thy names to tremble.

I am one of Thy handmaidens, O my Lord! I have turned my face towards the sanctuary of Thy gracious favors and the adored tabernacle of Thy glory. Purify me of all that is not of Thee, and strengthen me to love Thee and to fulfill Thy pleasure, that I may delight myself in the contemplation of Thy beauty, and be rid of all attachment to any of Thy creatures, and may, at every moment, proclaim: "Magnified be God, the Lord of the worlds!"

Let my food, O my Lord, be Thy beauty, and my drink the light of Thy presence, and my hope Thy pleasure, and my work Thy praise, and my companion Thy remembrance, and my aid Thy sovereignty, and my dwelling-place Thy habitation, and my home the seat which Thou hast exalted above the limitations of them that are shut out as by a veil from Thee.

Thou art, in truth, the God of power, of strength and glory. —*Bahá'u'lláh*

Glory to Thee, O my God! One of Thy handmaidens, who hath believed in Thee and in Thy signs, hath entered beneath the shadow of the tree of Thy oneness. Give her to quaff, O my God, by Thy Name, the Manifest and the Hidden, of Thy choice sealed Wine that it may take her away from her own self, and make her to be entirely devoted to Thy remembrance, and wholly detached from any one beside Thee.

Now that Thou hast revealed unto her the knowledge of Thee, O my Lord, deny her not, by Thy bounty, Thy grace; and now that Thou hast called her unto Thyself, drive her not away from Thee, through Thy favor. Supply her, then, with that which excelleth all that can be found on Thine earth. Thou art, verily, the Most Bountiful, Whose grace is immense.

Wert Thou to bestow on one of Thy creatures what would equal the kingdoms of earth and heaven, it would still not diminish by even as much as an atom the immensity of Thy dominion. Far greater art Thou than the Great One men are wont to call Thee, for such a title is but one of Thy names all of which were created by a mere indication of Thy will.

There is no God but Thee, the God of power, the God of glory, the God of knowledge and wisdom.   —*Bahá'u'lláh*

Thou seest, O my God, how the wrongs committed by such of Thy creatures as have turned their backs to Thee have come in between Him in Whom Thy Godhead is manifest and Thy servants. Send down upon them, O my Lord, what will cause them to be busied with each others' concerns. Let, then, their violence be confined to their own selves, that the land and they that dwell therein may find peace.

One of Thy handmaidens, O my Lord, hath sought Thy face, and soared in the atmosphere of Thy pleasure. Withhold not from her, O my Lord, the things Thou didst ordain for the chosen ones among Thy handmaidens. Enable her, then, to be so attracted by Thine utterances that she will celebrate Thy praise amongst them.

Potent art Thou to do what pleaseth Thee. No God is there but Thee, the Almighty, Whose help is implored by all men.

—Bahá'u'lláh

O my Lord, my Beloved, my Desire! Befriend me in my loneliness and accompany me in my exile. Remove my sorrow. Cause me to be devoted to Thy beauty. Withdraw me from all else save Thee. Attract me through Thy fragrances of holiness.

Cause me to be associated in Thy Kingdom
with those who are severed from all else save
Thee, who long to serve Thy sacred threshold and who stand to work in Thy Cause.
Enable me to be one of Thy maidservants
who have attained to Thy good pleasure. Verily, Thou art the Gracious, the Generous.

— 'Abdu'l-Bahá

EXPECTANT MOTHERS

My Lord! My Lord! I praise Thee and I
thank Thee for that whereby Thou hast
favored Thine humble maidservant, Thy
slave beseeching and supplicating Thee, because Thou hast verily guided her unto
Thine obvious Kingdom and caused her to
hear Thine exalted Call in the contingent
world and to behold Thy Signs which prove
the appearance of Thy victorious reign over
all things.

O my Lord, I dedicate that which is in my
womb unto Thee. Then cause it to be a praise-

worthy child in Thy Kingdom and a fortunate one by Thy favor and Thy generosity; to develop and to grow up under the charge of Thine education. Verily, Thou art the Gracious! Verily, Thou art the Lord of Great Favor!

—*'Abdu'l-Bahá*

YOUTH

O Thou kind Lord! From the horizon of detachment Thou hast manifested souls that, even as the shining moon, shed radiance upon the realm of heart and soul, rid themselves from the attributes of the world of existence and hastened forth unto the kingdom of immortality. With a drop from the ocean of Thy loving-kindness Thou didst oft-times moisten the gardens of their hearts until they gained incomparable freshness and beauty. The holy fragrance of Thy divine unity was diffused far and wide, shedding its sweet savors over the entire world, causing the regions of the earth to be redolent with perfume.

Raise up then, O spirit of Purity, souls who, like those sanctified beings, will become free and pure, will adorn the world of being with a new raiment and a wondrous robe, will seek no one else but Thee, tread no path except the path of Thy good pleasure and will speak of naught but the mysteries of Thy Cause.

O Thou kind Lord! Grant that this youth may attain unto that which is the highest aspiration of the holy ones. Endow him with the wings of Thy strengthening grace—wings of detachment and divine aid—that he may soar thereby into the atmosphere of Thy tender mercy, be able to partake of Thy celestial bestowals, may become a sign of divine guidance and a standard of the Concourse on high. Thou art the Potent, the Powerful, the Seeing, the Hearing.   — *'Abdu'l-Bahá*

O Thou kind Lord! Graciously bestow a pair of heavenly wings unto each of these fledglings, and give them spiritual power that they may wing their flight through this limitless space and may soar to the heights of the Abhá Kingdom.

O Lord! Strengthen these fragile seedlings that each one may become a fruitful tree, verdant and flourishing. Render these souls victorious through the potency of Thy celestial hosts, that they may be able to crush the forces of error and ignorance and to unfurl the standard of fellowship and guidance amidst the people; that they may, even as the reviving breaths of the spring, refresh and quicken the trees of human souls and like unto vernal showers make the meads of that region green and fertile.

Thou art the Mighty and the Powerful; Thou art the Bestower and the All-Loving.

— 'Abdu'l-Bahá

O Thou kind Lord! Bestow heavenly confirmation upon this daughter of the kingdom, and graciously aid her that she may remain firm and steadfast in Thy Cause and that she may, even as a nightingale of the rose garden of mysteries, warble melodies in the Abhá Kingdom in the most wondrous tones, thereby bringing happiness to everyone. Make her exalted among the daughters of the kingdom and enable her to attain life eternal.

Thou art the Bestower, the All-Loving.

— 'Abdu'l-Bahá

O Lord! Make this youth radiant, and confer Thy bounty upon this poor creature. Bestow upon him knowledge, grant him added strength at the break of every morn and guard him within the shelter of Thy protection so that he may be freed from error, may devote himself to the service of Thy Cause, may guide the wayward, lead the hapless, free the captives and awaken the heedless, that all may be blessed with Thy remembrance and praise. Thou art the Mighty and the Powerful.   — 'Abdu'l-Bahá

Praise and glory be to Thee, O Lord my God! This is a choice sapling which Thou hast planted in the meads of Thy love and hast nurtured with the fingers of Thy Lordship. Thou hast watered it from the wellspring of everlasting life which streameth forth from the gardens of Thy oneness and Thou hast caused the clouds of Thy tender mercy to shower Thy favors upon it. It hath now grown and developed beneath the shelter of Thy blessings which are manifest from the Dayspring of Thy divine essence. It hath burst forth into leaves and blossoms, is laden with fruit through the providence of Thy wondrous gifts and bounties and is stirred by the fragrant breeze wafting from the direction of Thy loving-kindness.

O Lord! Cause this sapling to become verdant, fresh and flourishing by the outpourings of Thy special bounty and favor, wherewith Thou hast endued the tabernacles of holiness in Thy eternal Kingdom and hast adorned the essences of unity in the arena of reunion.

O Lord! Assist him through Thy strengthening grace which proceedeth from Thine invisible Kingdom, aid him with such hosts as are hidden from the eyes of Thy servants and grant that he may have a sure footing in Thy presence. Unloose his tongue to make mention of Thee and gladden his heart to celebrate Thy praise. Illumine his face in Thy Kingdom, prosper him in the realm above and graciously confirm him to serve Thy Cause.

Thou art the All-Powerful, the All-Glorious, the Omnipotent.

— 'Abdu'l-Bahá

OCCASIONAL PRAYERS

THE FAST

The Kitáb-i-Aqdas states: "We have commanded you to pray and fast from the beginning of maturity [15 years]; this is ordained by God, your Lord and the Lord of your forefathers. . . . The traveler, the ailing, those who are with child or giving suck, are not bound by the Fast. . . . Abstain from food and drink from sunrise to sundown, and beware lest desire deprive you of this grace that is appointed in the Book."

The period of the Fast is March 2 through March 20.

This is, O my God, the first of the days on which Thou hast bidden Thy loved ones to observe the Fast. I ask of Thee by Thy Self and by him who hath fasted out of love for Thee and for Thy good-pleasure—and not out of self and desire, nor out of fear of Thy wrath—and by Thy most excellent names and august attributes, to purify Thy servants from the love of aught except Thee and to draw them nigh unto the Dawning-Place of the lights of Thy countenance and the Seat of the throne of Thy oneness. Illumine their hearts, O my God, with the light of Thy knowledge and brighten their faces with the rays of the Daystar that shineth from the horizon of Thy Will. Potent art Thou to do what pleaseth Thee. No God is there but Thee, the All-Glorious, Whose help is implored by all men.

Assist them, O my God, to render Thee victorious and to exalt Thy Word. Suffer them, then, to become as hands of Thy Cause amongst Thy servants, and make them to be revealers of Thy religion and Thy signs amongst mankind, in such wise that the whole world may be filled with Thy remembrance and praise and with Thy proofs and evidences. Thou art, verily, the All-Bounteous, the Most Exalted, the Powerful, the Mighty, and the Merciful.

—*Bahá'u'lláh*

In the Name of Him Who hath been promised in the Books of God, the All-Know-

ing, the All-Informed! The days of fasting
have arrived wherein those servants who
circle round Thy throne and have attained
Thy presence have fasted. Say: O God of
names and creator of heaven and earth! I beg
of Thee by Thy Name, the All-Glorious, to
accept the fast of those who have fasted for
love of Thee and for the sake of Thy good-
pleasure and have carried out what Thou
hast bidden them in Thy Books and Tablets.
I beseech Thee by them to assist me in the
promotion of Thy Cause and to make me
steadfast in Thy love, that my footsteps may
not slip on account of the clamor of Thy
creatures. Verily, Thou art powerful over
whatsoever Thou willest. No God is there
but Thee, the Quickener, the All-Powerful,
the Most Bountiful, the Ancient of Days.

—*Bahá'u'lláh*

I beseech Thee, O my God, by Thy mighty
Sign, and by the revelation of Thy grace
amongst men, to cast me not away from the
gate of the city of Thy presence, and to disappoint not the hopes I have set on the mani-

festations of Thy grace amidst Thy creatures. Thou seest me, O my God, holding to Thy Name, the Most Holy, the Most Luminous, the Most Mighty, the Most Great, the Most Exalted, the Most Glorious, and clinging to the hem of the robe to which have clung all in this world and in the world to come.

I beseech Thee, O my God, by Thy most sweet Voice and by Thy most exalted Word, to draw me ever nearer to the threshold of Thy door, and to suffer me not to be far removed from the shadow of Thy mercy and the canopy of Thy bounty. Thou seest me, O my God, holding to Thy Name, the Most Holy, the Most Luminous, the Most Mighty, the Most Great, the Most Exalted, the Most Glorious, and clinging to the hem of the robe to which have clung all in this world and in the world to come.

I beseech Thee, O my God, by the splendor of Thy luminous brow and the brightness of the light of Thy countenance, which shineth from the all-highest horizon, to attract me by the fragrance of Thy raiment, and make me drink of the choice wine of Thine utterance. Thou seest me, O my God, holding to Thy

Name, the Most Holy, the Most Luminous, the Most Mighty, the Most Great, the Most Exalted, the Most Glorious, and clinging to the hem of the robe to which have clung all in this world and in the world to come.

I beseech Thee, O my God, by Thy hair which moveth across Thy face, even as Thy most exalted pen moveth across the pages of Thy Tablets, shedding the musk of hidden meanings over the kingdom of Thy creation, so to raise me up to serve Thy Cause that I shall not fall back, nor be hindered by the suggestions of them who have caviled at Thy signs and turned away from Thy face. Thou seest me, O my God, holding to Thy Name, the Most Holy, the Most Luminous, the Most Mighty, the Most Great, the Most Exalted, the Most Glorious, and clinging to the hem of the robe to which have clung all in this world and in the world to come.

I beseech Thee, O my God, by Thy Name which Thou hast made the King of Names, by which all who are in heaven and all who are on earth have been enraptured, to enable me to gaze on the Daystar of Thy Beauty, and to supply me with the wine of Thine utterance. Thou seest me, O my God, holding to Thy Name, the Most Holy, the Most Luminous, the Most Mighty, the Most Great, the Most Exalted, the Most Glorious, and clinging to the hem of the robe to which have clung all in this world and in the world to come.

I beseech Thee, O my God, by the Tabernacle of Thy majesty upon the loftiest summits, and the Canopy of Thy Revelation on the highest hills, to graciously aid me to do what Thy will hath desired and Thy purpose hath manifested. Thou seest me, O my God, holding to Thy Name, the Most Holy, the Most Luminous, the Most Mighty, the Most Great, the Most Exalted, the Most Glorious, and clinging to the hem of the robe to which have clung all in this world and in the world to come.

I beseech Thee, O my God, by Thy Beauty that shineth forth above the horizon of eternity, a Beauty before which, as soon as it revealeth itself, the kingdom of beauty boweth down in worship, magnifying it in ringing tones, to grant that I may die to all that I possess and live to whatsoever belongeth unto

Thee. Thou seest me, O my God, holding to Thy Name, the Most Holy, the Most Luminous, the Most Mighty, the Most Great, the Most Exalted, the Most Glorious, and clinging to the hem of the robe to which have clung all in this world and in the world to come.

I beseech Thee, O my God, by the Manifestation of Thy name, the Well-Beloved, through Whom the hearts of Thy lovers were consumed and the souls of all that dwell on earth have soared aloft, to aid me to remember Thee amongst Thy creatures, and to extol Thee amidst Thy people. Thou seest me, O my God, holding to Thy Name, the Most Holy, the Most Luminous, the Most Mighty, the Most Great, the Most Exalted, the Most Glorious, and clinging to the hem of the robe to which have clung all in this world and in the world to come.

I beseech Thee, O my God, by the rustling of the Divine Lote-Tree and the murmur of the breezes of Thine utterance in the kingdom of Thy names, to remove me far from whatsoever Thy will abhorreth, and draw me nigh unto the station wherein He Who is the Dayspring of Thy signs hath shone forth. Thou seest me, O my God, holding to Thy Name, the Most Holy, the Most Luminous, the Most Mighty, the Most Great, the Most Exalted, the Most Glorious, and clinging to the hem of the robe to which have clung all in this world and in the world to come.

I beseech Thee, O my God, by that Letter which, as soon as it proceeded out of the mouth of Thy will, hath caused the oceans to surge, and the winds to blow, and the fruits to be revealed, and the trees to spring forth, and all past traces to vanish, and all veils to be rent asunder, and them who are devoted to Thee to hasten unto the light of the countenance of their Lord, the Unconstrained, to make known unto me what lay hid in the treasuries of Thy knowledge and concealed within the repositories of Thy wisdom. Thou seest me, O my God, holding to Thy Name, the Most Holy, the Most Luminous, the Most Mighty, the Most Great, the Most Exalted, the Most Glorious, and clinging to the hem of the robe to which have clung all in this world and in the world to come.

I beseech Thee, O my God, by the fire of Thy love which drove sleep from the eyes of

Thy chosen ones and Thy loved ones, and by their remembrance and praise of Thee at the hour of dawn, to number me with such as have attained unto that which Thou hast sent down in Thy Book and manifested through Thy will. Thou seest me, O my God, holding to Thy Name, the Most Holy, the Most Luminous, the Most Mighty, the Most Great, the Most Exalted, the Most Glorious, and clinging to the hem of the robe to which have clung all in this world and in the world to come.

I beseech Thee, O my God, by the light of Thy countenance which impelled them who are nigh unto Thee to meet the darts of Thy decree, and such as are devoted to Thee to face the swords of Thine enemies in Thy path, to write down for me with Thy most exalted Pen what Thou hast written down for Thy trusted ones and Thy chosen ones. Thou seest me, O my God, holding to Thy Name, the Most Holy, the Most Luminous, the Most Mighty, the Most Great, the Most Exalted, the Most Glorious, and clinging to the hem of the robe to which have clung all in this world and in the world to come.

I beseech Thee, O my God, by Thy Name through which Thou hast hearkened unto the call of Thy lovers, and the sighs of them that long for Thee, and the cry of them that enjoy near access to Thee, and the groaning of them that are devoted to Thee, and through which Thou hast fulfilled the wishes of them that have set their hopes on Thee, and hast granted them their desires, through Thy grace and Thy favors, and by Thy Name through which the ocean of forgiveness surged before Thy face, and the clouds of Thy generosity rained upon Thy servants, to write down for everyone who hath turned unto Thee, and observed the Fast prescribed by Thee, the recompense decreed for such as speak not except by Thy leave, and who forsook all that they possessed in Thy path and for love of Thee.

I beseech Thee, O my Lord, by Thyself, and by Thy signs, and Thy clear tokens, and the shining light of the Daystar of Thy Beauty, and Thy Branches, to cancel the trespasses of those who have held fast to Thy laws, and have observed what Thou hast prescribed unto them in Thy Book. Thou seest me, O my God, hold-

ing to Thy Name, the Most Holy, the Most
Luminous, the Most Mighty, the Most Great,
the Most Exalted, the Most Glorious, and clinging to the hem of the robe to which have clung
all in this world and in the world to come.

— *Bahá'u'lláh*

Praise be to Thee, O Lord my God! I beseech Thee by this Revelation whereby
darkness hath been turned into light,
through which the Frequented Fane hath
been built, and the Written Tablet revealed,
and the Outspread Roll uncovered, to send
down upon me and upon them who are in
my company that which will enable us to
soar into the heavens of Thy transcendent
glory, and will wash us from the stain of such
doubts as have hindered the suspicious from
entering into the tabernacle of Thy unity.

I am the one, O my Lord, who hath held
fast the cord of Thy loving-kindness, and clung
to the hem of Thy mercy and favors. Do Thou
ordain for me and for my loved ones the good
of this world and of the world to come. Supply

them, then, with the Hidden Gift Thou didst ordain for the choicest among Thy creatures.

These are, O my Lord, the days in which Thou hast bidden Thy servants to observe the Fast. Blessed is he that observeth the Fast wholly for Thy sake and with absolute detachment from all things except Thee. Assist me and assist them, O my Lord, to obey Thee and to keep Thy precepts. Thou, verily, hast power to do what Thou choosest.

There is no God but Thee, the All-Knowing, the All-Wise. All praise be to God, the Lord of all worlds.   —*Bahá'u'lláh*

These are, O my God, the days whereon Thou didst enjoin Thy servants to observe the Fast. With it Thou didst adorn the preamble of the Book of Thy Laws revealed unto Thy creatures, and didst deck forth the Repositories of Thy commandments in the sight of all who are in Thy heaven and all who are on Thy earth. Thou hast endowed every hour of these days with a special virtue, inscrutable to all except Thee, Whose knowledge embraceth all created things. Thou hast, also, assigned unto every soul a portion of this virtue in accordance with the Tablet of Thy decree and the Scriptures of Thine irrevocable judgment. Every leaf of these Books and Scriptures Thou hast, moreover, allotted to each one of the peoples and kindreds of the earth.

For Thine ardent lovers Thou hast, according to Thy decree, reserved, at each daybreak, the cup of Thy remembrance, O Thou Who art the Ruler of rulers! These are they who have been so inebriated with the wine of Thy manifold wisdom that they forsake their couches in their longing to celebrate Thy praise and extol Thy virtues, and flee from sleep in their eagerness to approach Thy presence and partake of Thy bounty. Their eyes have, at all times, been bent upon the Dayspring of Thy loving-kindness, and their faces set towards the Fountainhead of Thine inspiration. Rain down, then, upon us and upon them from the clouds of Thy mercy what beseemeth the heaven of Thy bounteousness and grace.

Lauded be Thy name, O my God! This is the hour when Thou hast unlocked the doors of Thy bounty before the faces of Thy creatures, and opened wide the portals of Thy tender mercy unto all the dwellers of Thine earth. I beseech Thee, by all them whose blood was shed in Thy path, who, in their yearning over Thee, rid themselves from all attachment to any of Thy creatures, and who were so carried away by the sweet savors of Thine inspiration that every single member of their bodies intoned Thy praise and vibrated to Thy remembrance, not to withhold from us the things Thou hast irrevocably ordained in this Revelation—a Revelation the potency of which hath caused every tree to cry out what the Burning Bush had aforetime proclaimed unto Moses, Who conversed with Thee, a Revelation that hath enabled every least pebble to resound again with Thy praise, as the stones glorified Thee in the days of Muḥammad, Thy Friend.

These are the ones, O my God, whom Thou hast graciously enabled to have fellowship with Thee and to commune with Him Who is the Revealer of Thyself. The winds of Thy will have scattered them abroad until Thou didst gather them together beneath Thy shadow, and didst cause them to enter into the precincts of Thy court. Now that Thou hast made them to abide under the shade of the canopy of Thy mercy, do Thou assist them to attain what must befit so august a station. Suffer them not, O my Lord, to be numbered with them who, though enjoying near access to Thee, have been kept back from recognizing Thy face, and who, though meeting with Thee, are deprived of Thy presence.

These are Thy servants, O my Lord, who have entered with Thee in this, the Most Great Prison, who have kept the Fast within its walls according to what Thou hast commanded them in the Tablets of Thy decree and the Books of Thy behest. Send down, therefore, upon them what will thoroughly purge them of all that Thou abhorrest, that they may be wholly devoted to Thee, and may detach themselves entirely from all except Thyself.

Rain down, then, upon us, O my God, that which beseemeth Thy grace and befitteth Thy bounty. Enable us, then, O my God, to live in remembrance of Thee and to die in love of Thee, and supply us with the gift of Thy presence in Thy worlds hereafter—worlds which are inscrutable to all except Thee. Thou art our Lord and the Lord of all worlds, and the God of all that are in heaven and all that are on earth.

Thou beholdest, O my God, what hath befallen Thy dear ones in Thy days. Thy glory beareth me witness! The voice of the lamentation of Thy chosen ones hath been lifted up throughout Thy realm. Some were ensnared by the infidels in Thy land, and were hindered by them from having near access to Thee and from attaining the court of Thy glory. Others were able to approach Thee, but were kept back from beholding Thy face. Still others were permitted, in their eagerness to look upon Thee, to enter the precincts of Thy court, but they allowed the veils of the imaginations of Thy creatures and the wrongs inflicted by the oppressors among Thy people to come in between them and Thee.

This is the hour, O my Lord, which Thou hast caused to excel every other hour, and hast related to the choicest among Thy creatures. I beseech Thee, O my God, by Thy Self and by them, to ordain in the course of this year what

shall exalt Thy loved ones. Do Thou, moreover, decree within this year what will enable
the Daystar of Thy power to shine brightly
above the horizon of Thy glory, and to illumi-
nate by Thy sovereign might, the whole world.

Render Thy Cause victorious, O my Lord,
and abase Thou Thine enemies. Write down,
then, for us the good of this life and of the life
to come. Thou art the Truth, Who knoweth
the secret things. No God is there but Thee,
the Ever-Forgiving, the All-Bountiful.

—*Bahá'u'lláh*

Glory be to Thee, O Lord my God! These
are the days whereon Thou hast bidden
all men to observe the Fast, that through it
they may purify their souls and rid themselves of all attachment to anyone but Thee,
and that out of their hearts may ascend that
which will be worthy of the court of Thy
majesty and may well beseem the seat of the
revelation of Thy oneness. Grant, O my
Lord, that this fast may become a river of
life-giving waters and may yield the virtue
wherewith Thou hast endowed it. Cleanse

Thou by its means the hearts of Thy servants whom the evils of the world have failed to hinder from turning towards Thine all-glorious Name, and who have remained unmoved by the noise and tumult of such as have repudiated Thy most resplendent signs which have accompanied the advent of Thy Manifestation Whom Thou hast invested with Thy sovereignty, Thy power, Thy majesty and glory. These are the servants who, as soon as Thy call reached them, hastened in the direction of Thy mercy and were not kept back from Thee by the changes and chances of this world or by any human limitations.

I am he, O my God, who testifieth to Thy unity, who acknowledgeth Thy oneness, who boweth humbly before the revelations of Thy majesty, and who recognizeth with downcast countenance the splendors of the light of Thy transcendent glory. I have believed in Thee after Thou didst enable me to know Thy Self, Whom Thou hast revealed to men's eyes through the power of Thy sovereignty and might. Unto Him I have turned, wholly de-

tached from all things, and cleaving steadfastly
unto the cord of Thy gifts and favors. I have
embraced His truth, and the truth of all the
wondrous laws and precepts that have been sent
down unto Him. I have fasted for love of Thee
and in pursuance of Thine injunction, and have
broken my fast with Thy praise on my tongue
and in conformity with Thy pleasure. Suffer
me not, O my Lord, to be reckoned among
them who have fasted in the daytime, who in
the night-season have prostrated themselves
before Thy face, and who have repudiated Thy
truth, disbelieved in Thy signs, gainsaid Thy
testimony, and perverted Thine utterances.

Open Thou, O my Lord, mine eyes and the
eyes of all them that have sought Thee, that
we may recognize Thee with Thine own eyes.
This is Thy bidding given us in the Book sent
down by Thee unto Him Whom Thou hast
chosen by Thy behest, Whom Thou hast
singled out for Thy favor above all Thy creatures, Whom Thou hast been pleased to invest
with Thy sovereignty, and Whom Thou hast
specially favored and entrusted with Thy Message unto Thy people. Praised be Thou, there-

fore, O my God, inasmuch as Thou hast graciously enabled us to recognize Him and to acknowledge whatsoever hath been sent down unto Him, and conferred upon us the honor of attaining the presence of the One Whom Thou didst promise in Thy Book and in Thy Tablets.

Thou seest me then, O my God, with my face turned towards Thee, cleaving steadfastly to the cord of Thy gracious providence and generosity, and clinging to the hem of Thy tender mercies and bountiful favors. Destroy not, I implore Thee, my hopes of attaining unto that which Thou didst ordain for Thy servants who have turned towards the precincts of Thy court and the sanctuary of Thy presence, and have observed the Fast for love of Thee. I confess, O my God, that whatever proceedeth from me is wholly unworthy of Thy sovereignty and falleth short of Thy majesty. And yet I beseech Thee by Thy Name through which Thou hast revealed Thy Self, in the glory of Thy most excellent titles, unto all created things, in this Revelation whereby Thou hast, through Thy most resplendent Name, manifested Thy beauty, to give me to drink of the wine of Thy mercy and of the pure beverage of Thy favor, which have streamed forth from the right hand of Thy will, that I may so fix my gaze upon Thee and be so detached from all else but Thee, that the world and all that hath been created therein may appear before me as a fleeting day which Thou hast not deigned to create.

I moreover entreat Thee, O my God, to rain down, from the heaven of Thy will and the clouds of Thy mercy, that which will cleanse us from the noisome savors of our transgressions, O Thou Who hast called Thyself the God of Mercy! Thou art, verily, the Most Powerful, the All-Glorious, the Beneficent.

Cast not away, O my Lord, him that hath turned towards Thee, nor suffer him who hath drawn nigh unto Thee to be removed far from Thy court. Dash not the hopes of the suppliant who hath longingly stretched out his hands to seek Thy grace and favors, and deprive not Thy sincere servants of the wonders of Thy tender mercies and loving-kindness. Forgiving and Most Bountiful art Thou, O my Lord! Power hast Thou to do what Thou pleasest. All else but Thee are impotent before the revelations of Thy might, are as lost in the face of the evidences of Thy wealth, are as nothing when compared with the manifestations of Thy transcendent sovereignty, and are destitute of all strength when face to face with the signs and tokens of Thy power. What refuge is there beside Thee, O my Lord, to which I can flee, and where is there a haven to which I can hasten? Nay, the power of Thy might beareth me witness! No protector is there but Thee, no place to flee to except Thee, no refuge to seek save Thee. Cause me to taste, O my Lord, the divine sweetness of Thy remembrance and praise. I swear by Thy might! Whosoever tasteth of its sweetness will rid himself of all attachment to the world and all that is therein, and will set his face towards Thee, cleansed from the remembrance of anyone except Thee.

Inspire then my soul, O my God, with Thy wondrous remembrance, that I may glorify Thy name. Number me not with them who read Thy words and fail to find Thy hidden gift which, as decreed by Thee, is contained therein, and which quickeneth the souls of Thy creatures and the hearts of Thy servants. Cause me,

O my Lord, to be reckoned among them who have been so stirred up by the sweet savors that have been wafted in Thy days that they have laid down their lives for Thee and hastened to the scene of their death in their longing to gaze on Thy beauty and in their yearning to attain Thy presence. And were anyone to say unto them on their way, "Whither go ye?" they would say, "Unto God, the All-Possessing, the Help in Peril, the Self-Subsisting!"

The transgressions committed by such as have turned away from Thee and have borne themselves haughtily towards Thee have not availed to hinder them from loving Thee, and from setting their faces towards Thee, and from turning in the direction of Thy mercy. These are they who are blessed by the Concourse on high, who are glorified by the denizens of the everlasting Cities, and beyond them by those on whose foreheads Thy most exalted pen hath written: "These! The people of Bahá. Through them have been shed the splendors of the light of guidance." Thus hath it been ordained, at Thy behest and by Thy will, in the Tablet of Thine irrevocable decree.

Proclaim, therefore, O my God, their greatness and the greatness of those who while living or after death have circled round them. Supply them with that which Thou hast ordained for the righteous among Thy creatures. Potent art Thou to do all things. There is no God but Thee, the All-Powerful, the Help in Peril, the Almighty, the Most Bountiful.

Do not bring our fasts to an end with this fast, O my Lord, nor the covenants Thou hast made with this covenant. Do Thou accept all that we have done for love of Thee, and for the sake of Thy pleasure, and all that we have left undone as a result of our subjection to our evil and corrupt desires. Enable us, then, to cleave steadfastly to Thy love and Thy good pleasure, and preserve us from the mischief of such as have denied Thee and repudiated Thy most resplendent signs. Thou art, in truth, the Lord of this world and of the next. No God is there beside Thee, the Exalted, the Most High.

Magnify Thou, O Lord my God, Him Who is the Primal Point, the Divine Mystery, the Unseen Essence, the Dayspring of Divinity, and the Manifestation of Thy Lordship, through Whom all the knowledge of the past and all

the knowledge of the future were made plain,
through Whom the pearls of Thy hidden wisdom were uncovered, and the mystery of Thy
treasured name disclosed, Whom Thou hast
appointed as the Announcer of the One
through Whose name the letter B and the letter E have been joined and united, through
Whom Thy majesty, Thy sovereignty and Thy
might were made known, through Whom Thy
words have been sent down, and Thy laws set
forth with clearness, and Thy signs spread
abroad, and Thy Word established, through
Whom the hearts of Thy chosen ones were laid
bare, and all that were in the heavens and all
that were on the earth were gathered together,
Whom Thou hast called 'Alí-Muḥammad in the
kingdom of Thy names, and the Spirit of Spirits in the Tablets of Thine irrevocable decree,
Whom Thou hast invested with Thine own
title, unto Whose name all other names have,
at Thy bidding and through the power of Thy
might, been made to return, and in Whom
Thou hast caused all Thine attributes and titles
to attain their final consummation. To Him also
belong such names as lay hid within Thy stain-

less tabernacles, in Thine invisible world and Thy sanctified cities.

Magnify Thou, moreover, such as have believed in Him and in His signs and have turned towards Him, from among those that have acknowledged Thy unity in His Latter Manifestation—a Manifestation whereof He hath made mention in His Tablets, and in His Books, and in His Scriptures, and in all the wondrous verses and gem-like utterances that have descended upon Him. It is this same Manifestation Whose covenant Thou hast bidden Him establish ere He had established His own covenant. He it is Whose praise the Bayán hath celebrated. In it His excellence hath been extolled, and His truth established, and His sovereignty proclaimed, and His Cause perfected. Blessed is the man that hath turned unto Him, and fulfilled the things He hath commanded, O Thou Who art the Lord of the world and the Desire of all them that have known Thee!

Praised be Thou, O my God, inasmuch as Thou hast aided us to recognize and love Him. I, therefore, beseech Thee by Him and by Them Who are the Daysprings of Thy Divinity, and the Manifestations of Thy Lordship, and the

Treasuries of Thy Revelation, and the Depositories of Thine inspiration, to enable us to serve and obey Him, and to empower us to become the helpers of His Cause and the dispersers of His adversaries. Powerful art Thou to do all that pleaseth Thee. No God is there beside Thee, the Almighty, the All-Glorious, the One Whose help is sought by all men!

—*Bahá'u'lláh*

Praise be unto Thee, O Lord my God! We have observed the Fast in conformity with Thy bidding and break it now through Thy love and Thy good-pleasure. Deign to accept, O my God, the deeds that we have performed in Thy path wholly for the sake of Thy beauty with our faces set towards Thy Cause, free from aught else but Thee. Bestow, then, Thy forgiveness upon us, upon our forefathers, and upon all such as have believed in Thee and in Thy mighty signs in this most great, this most glorious Revelation. Potent art Thou to do what Thou choosest. Thou art, verily, the Most Exalted, the Almighty, the Unconstrained.

—*Bahá'u'lláh*

Praised be Thou, O God, my God! These are the days whereon Thou hast enjoined Thy chosen ones, Thy loved ones and Thy servants to observe the Fast, which Thou hast made a light unto the people of Thy kingdom, even as Thou didst make obligatory prayer a ladder of ascent unto those who acknowledge Thy unity. I beg of Thee, O my God, by these two mighty pillars, which Thou hast ordained as a glory and honor for all mankind, to keep Thy religion safe from the mischief of the ungodly and the plotting of every wicked doer. O Lord, conceal not the light which Thou hast revealed through Thy strength and Thine omnipotence. Assist, then, those who truly believe in Thee with the hosts of the seen and the unseen by Thy command and Thy sovereignty. No God is there but Thee, the Almighty, the Most Powerful.

—*Bahá'u'lláh*

ḤUQÚQU'LLÁH:
THE RIGHT OF GOD

Ḥuqúqu'lláh is indeed a great law. It is incumbent upon all to make this offering, because it is the source of grace, abundance, and of all good. It is a bounty which shall remain with every soul in every world of the worlds of God, the All-Possessing, the All-Bountiful.

—*Bahá'u'lláh*

Magnified art Thou, O Lord of the entire creation, the One unto Whom all things must turn. With my inner and outer tongues I bear witness that Thou hast manifested and revealed Thyself, sent down Thy signs, and proclaimed Thy testimonies. I testify to Thy self-sufficiency from aught else except Thee, and Thy sanctity above all earthly things. I entreat Thee by the transcendent glory of Thy Cause and the supreme potency of Thy Word to grant confir-

mation unto him who desireth to offer what
Thou hast prescribed unto him in Thy Book
and to observe that which will shed forth the
fragrance of Thine acceptance. Verily Thou
art the All-Mighty, the All-Gracious, the All-
Forgiving, the All-Generous.   —*Bahá'u'lláh*

Glorified art Thou, O my compassionate
Lord! I entreat Thee by the tumult of
the ocean of Thy holy utterance, and by the
manifold tokens of Thy supreme sovereignty, and the compelling evidences of Thy
Divinity, and the hidden mysteries that lie
concealed within Thy knowledge, to give me
Thy grace to serve Thee and Thy chosen
ones, and enable me to dutifully offer Thy
Ḥuqúq which Thou hast ordained in Thy
Book.

I am the one, O my Lord, who hath set his
affections on Thy realm of glory, and hath
clung tenaciously to the hem of Thy generosity. O Thou Who art the Lord of all being and
the Ruler of the kingdom of names, I beseech
Thee not to deny me the things Thou dost

possess, nor to withhold from me that which Thou hast ordained for Thy chosen ones.

I implore Thee, O Lord of all names and Creator of the heavens, to assist me to be steadfast in Thy Cause, through Thy strengthening grace, in such wise that the vanities of the world may not suffer me to be shut out as by a veil, nor to be hindered by the violent commotions of the wicked-doers who have risen up to lead Thy people astray in Thy days. Destine for me then, O my heart's Desire, the good of this world and the world to come. Verily Thou art powerful to do as Thou willest. No God is there but Thee, the Ever-Forgiving, the Most Generous. —*Bahá'u'lláh*

INTERCALARY DAYS

(The Intercalary Days, February 26 to March 1, inclusive, should be days of preparation for the Fast, days of hospitality, charity, and the giving of presents.)

My God, my Fire and my Light! The days which Thou hast named the Ayyám-i-Há* in Thy Book have begun, O Thou Who art the King of names, and the Fast which Thy most exalted Pen hath enjoined unto all who are in the kingdom of Thy creation to observe is approaching. I entreat Thee, O my Lord, by these days and by all such as have during that period clung to the cord of Thy commandments, and laid hold on the handle of Thy precepts, to grant that unto every soul may be assigned a place within the pre-

* The Days of Há, Intercalary Days.

cincts of Thy court, and a seat at the revelation of the splendors of the light of Thy countenance.

These, O my Lord, are Thy servants whom no corrupt inclination hath kept back from what Thou didst send down in Thy Book. They have bowed themselves before Thy Cause, and received Thy Book with such resolve as is born of Thee, and observed what Thou hadst prescribed unto them, and chosen to follow that which had been sent down by Thee.

Thou seest, O my Lord, how they have recognized and confessed whatsoever Thou hast revealed in Thy Scriptures. Give them to drink, O my Lord, from the hands of Thy graciousness the waters of Thine eternity. Write down, then, for them the recompense ordained for him that hath immersed himself in the ocean of Thy presence, and attained unto the choice wine of Thy meeting.

I implore Thee, O Thou the King of kings and the Pitier of the downtrodden, to ordain for them the good of this world and of the world to come. Write down for them, moreover, what none of Thy creatures hath discovered, and number them with those who have circled round Thee, and who move about Thy throne in every world of Thy worlds.

Thou, truly, art the Almighty, the All-Knowing, the All-Informed. —*Bahá'u'lláh*

MARTYRS AND THEIR FAMILIES

He is God!

O Lord my God! O Thou Helper of the feeble, Succorer of the poor and Deliverer of the helpless who turn unto Thee.

With utmost lowliness I raise my suppliant hands to Thy kingdom of beauty and fervently call upon Thee with my inner tongue, saying: O God, my God! Aid me to adore Thee, strengthen my loins to serve Thee; assist me by Thy grace in my servitude to Thee; suffer me to remain steadfast in my obedience to Thee; pour forth upon me the liberal effusions of Thy bounty, let the glances of the eye of Thy loving-kindness be directed towards me, and immerse me in the ocean of Thy forgiveness. Grant that I may be confirmed in my allegiance to Thy Faith, and bestow upon me a fuller measure of certitude and assurance, that I may wholly dispense with the world, may turn my face with entire devotion towards Thy face, be reinforced by the compelling power of proofs and testimonies, and, invested with majesty and power, may pass beyond every region of heaven and earth. Verily Thou art the Merciful, the All-Glorious, the Kind, the Compassionate.

O Lord! These are the survivors of the martyrs, that company of blessed souls. They have sustained every tribulation and displayed patience in the face of grievous injustice. They have forsaken all comfort and prosperity, have willingly submitted to dire suffering and adversity in the path of Thy love, and are still held captive in the clutches of their enemies who continually torment them with sore torment, and oppress them because they walk steadfastly in Thy straight path. There is no one to help them, no one to befriend them. Apart from the ignoble and the wicked, there is no one to associate and consort with them.

O Lord! These souls have tasted bitter agony in this earthly life and have, as a sign of their

love for the shining beauty of Thy countenance
and in their eagerness to attain Thy celestial
kingdom, tolerated every gross indignity that
the people of tyranny have inflicted upon them.

O Lord! Fill their ears with the verses of divine assistance and of a speedy victory, and
deliver them from the oppression of such as
wield terrible might. Withhold the hands of
the wicked and leave not these souls to be torn
by the claws and teeth of fierce beasts, for they
are captivated by their love for Thee, entrusted
with the mysteries of Thy holiness, stand humbly at Thy door and have attained to Thine
exalted precinct.

O Lord! Graciously reinforce them with a
new spirit; illumine their eyes by enabling them
to behold Thy wondrous evidences in the
gloom of night; destine for them all good that
aboundeth in Thy Kingdom of eternal mysteries; make them as brilliant stars shining over
all regions, luxuriant trees laden with fruit and
branches moving in the breezes of dawn.

Verily, Thou art the Bountiful, the Mighty,
the Omnipotent, the Unconstrained. There is
none other God but Thee, the God of love and

tender mercy, the All-Glorious, the Ever-Forgiving.   —*'Abdu'l-Bahá*

NAW-RÚZ

(Naw-Rúz, March 21, is the first day of the Bahá'í year.)

Praised be Thou, O my God, that Thou hast ordained Naw-Rúz as a festival unto those who have observed the Fast for love of Thee and abstained from all that is abhorrent unto Thee. Grant, O my Lord, that the fire of Thy love and the heat produced by the Fast enjoined by Thee may inflame them in Thy Cause, and make them to be occupied with Thy praise and with remembrance of Thee.

Since Thou hast adorned them, O my Lord, with the ornament of the Fast prescribed by Thee, do Thou adorn them also with the ornament of Thine acceptance, through Thy grace and bountiful favor. For the doings of men are all dependent upon Thy good pleasure, and are conditioned by Thy behest. Shouldst Thou regard him who hath broken the Fast as one who hath observed it, such a man would be reckoned among them who from eternity had been keeping the Fast. And shouldst Thou decree that he who hath observed the Fast hath broken it, that person would be numbered with such as have caused the Robe of Thy Revelation to be stained with dust, and been far removed from the crystal waters of this living Fountain.

Thou art He through Whom the ensign "Praiseworthy art Thou in Thy works" hath been lifted up, and the standard "Obeyed art Thou in Thy behest" hath been unfurled. Make known this Thy station, O my God, unto Thy servants, that they may be made aware that the excellence of all things is dependent upon Thy bidding and Thy word, and the virtue of every act is conditioned by Thy leave and the good pleasure of Thy will, and may recognize that the reins of men's doings are within the grasp of Thine acceptance and Thy commandment. Make this known unto them, that nothing whatsoever may shut them out from Thy Beauty, in these days whereon the Christ exclaimeth: "All dominion is Thine, O Thou the Begetter of the Spirit (Jesus)"; and Thy Friend (Muḥammad) crieth out: "Glory be to Thee, O Thou the Best-Beloved, for that Thou hast uncovered Thy Beauty, and written down for Thy chosen ones what will cause them to attain unto the seat of the revelation of Thy Most Great Name, through which all the peoples have lamented except such as have detached themselves from all else except Thee, and set themselves towards Him Who is the Revealer of Thyself and the Manifestation of Thine attributes."

He Who is Thy Branch and all Thy company, O my Lord, have broken this day their fast, after having observed it within the precincts of Thy court, and in their eagerness to please Thee. Do Thou ordain for Him, and for them, and for all such as have entered Thy presence in those days all the good Thou didst destine in Thy Book. Supply them, then, with that which will profit them, in both this life and in the life beyond.

Thou, in truth, art the All-Knowing, the All-Wise.   —Bahá'u'lláh

SPIRITUAL ASSEMBLY

Whenever ye enter the council-chamber, recite this prayer with a heart throbbing with the love of God and a tongue purified from all but His remembrance, that the All-Powerful may graciously aid you to achieve supreme victory.

O God, my God! We are servants of Thine that have turned with devotion to Thy Holy Face, that have detached ourselves from all besides Thee in this glorious Day. We have gathered in this Spiritual Assembly, united in our views and thoughts, with our purposes harmonized to exalt Thy Word amidst mankind. O Lord, our God! Make us the signs of Thy Divine Guidance, the Standards of Thine exalted Faith amongst men, servants to Thy mighty Covenant, O Thou our Lord Most High, manifestations of Thy Divine Unity in Thine Abhá Kingdom, and resplendent stars shin-

ing upon all regions. Lord! Aid us to become
seas surging with the billows of Thy wondrous Grace, streams flowing from Thine all-
glorious Heights, goodly fruits upon the Tree
of Thy heavenly Cause, trees waving through
the breezes of Thy Bounty in Thy celestial
Vineyard. O God! Make our souls dependent
upon the Verses of Thy Divine Unity, our
hearts cheered with the outpourings of Thy
Grace, that we may unite even as the waves
of one sea and become merged together as
the rays of Thine effulgent Light; that our
thoughts, our views, our feelings may become as one reality, manifesting the spirit of
union throughout the world. Thou art the
Gracious, the Bountiful, the Bestower, the
Almighty, the Merciful, the Compassionate.

— 'Abdu'l-Bahá

*Come ye together in gladness unalloyed, and at the be-
ginning of the meeting, recite ye this prayer:*

O Thou Lord of the Kingdom! Though
our bodies be gathered here together,
yet our spellbound hearts are carried away by

Thy love, and yet are we transported by the rays of Thy resplendent face. Weak though we be, we await the revelations of Thy might and power. Poor though we be, with neither goods nor means, still take we riches from the treasures of Thy Kingdom. Drops though we be, still do we draw from out Thy ocean deeps. Motes though we be, still do we gleam in the glory of Thy splendid Sun.

O Thou our Provider! Send down Thine aid, that each one gathered here may become a lighted candle, each one a center of attraction, each one a summoner to Thy heavenly realms, till at last we make this nether world the mirror image of Thy Paradise.   —'Abdu'l-Bahá

Prayer to be said at the close of the meeting of the Spiritual Assembly.

O God! O God! From the unseen kingdom of Thy oneness behold us assembled in this spiritual meeting, believing in Thee, confident in Thy signs, firm in Thy

Covenant and Testament, attracted to Thee, set aglow with the fire of Thy love and sincere in Thy Cause. We are servants in Thy vineyard, spreaders of Thy religion, devoted worshipers of Thy countenance, humble towards Thy loved ones, submissive before Thy door, and imploring Thee to confirm us in serving Thy chosen ones, to support us with Thine unseen hosts, to strengthen our loins in Thy servitude and to make us submissive and adoring subjects communing with Thee.

O our Lord! We are weak, and Thou art the Mighty, the Powerful. We are lifeless, and Thou art the great life-giving Spirit. We are needy, and Thou art the Sustainer, the Powerful.

O our Lord! Turn our faces unto Thy merciful countenance, feed us from Thy heavenly table with Thine abundant grace, assist us with the hosts of Thy supreme angels and confirm us through the holy ones of the Kingdom of Abhá.

Verily, Thou art the Generous, the Merciful. Thou art the Possessor of great bounty, and, verily, Thou art the Clement and the Gracious.

—'Abdu'l-Bahá

SPECIAL TABLETS

TABLET OF AḤMAD

"These daily obligatory prayers, together with a few other specific ones, such as the Healing Prayer, the Tablet of Aḥmad, have been invested by Bahá'u'lláh with a special potency and significance, and should therefore be accepted as such and be recited by the believers with unquestioning faith and confidence, that through them they may enter into a much closer communion with God, and identify themselves more fully with His laws and precepts."
—From a letter written on behalf of Shoghi Effendi

He is the King, the All-Knowing, the Wise!

Lo, the Nightingale of Paradise singeth upon the twigs of the Tree of Eternity, with holy and sweet melodies, proclaiming to the sincere ones the glad tidings of the nearness of God, calling the believers in the Divine Unity to the court of the Presence of the Generous One, informing the severed ones of the message

307

which hath been revealed by God, the King, the Glorious, the Peerless, guiding the lovers to the seat of sanctity and to this resplendent Beauty.

Verily this is that Most Great Beauty, foretold in the Books of the Messengers, through Whom truth shall be distinguished from error and the wisdom of every command shall be tested. Verily He is the Tree of Life that bringeth forth the fruits of God, the Exalted, the Powerful, the Great.

O Aḥmad! Bear thou witness that verily He is God and there is no God but Him, the King, the Protector, the Incomparable, the Omnipotent. And that the One Whom He hath sent forth by the name of ‘Alí* was the true One from God, to Whose commands we are all conforming.

Say: O people be obedient to the ordinances of God, which have been enjoined in the Bayán by the Glorious, the Wise One. Verily He is the King of the Messengers and His Book is the Mother Book did ye but know.

* The Báb.

Thus doth the Nightingale utter His call unto you from this prison. He hath but to deliver this clear message. Whosoever desireth, let him turn aside from this counsel and whosoever desireth let him choose the path to his Lord.

O people, if ye deny these verses, by what proof have ye believed in God? Produce it, O assemblage of false ones.

Nay, by the One in Whose hand is my soul, they are not, and never shall be able to do this, even should they combine to assist one another.

O Aḥmad! Forget not My bounties while I am absent. Remember My days during thy days, and My distress and banishment in this remote prison. And be thou so steadfast in My love that thy heart shall not waver, even if the swords of the enemies rain blows upon thee and all the heavens and the earth arise against thee.

Be thou as a flame of fire to My enemies and a river of life eternal to My loved ones, and be not of those who doubt.

And if thou art overtaken by affliction in My path, or degradation for My sake, be not thou troubled thereby.

Rely upon God, thy God and the Lord of thy fathers. For the people are wandering in the paths of delusion, bereft of discernment to see God with their own eyes, or hear His Melody with their own ears. Thus have We found them, as thou also dost witness.

Thus have their superstitions become veils between them and their own hearts and kept them from the path of God, the Exalted, the Great.

Be thou assured in thyself that verily, he who turneth away from this Beauty hath also turned away from the Messengers of the past and showeth pride towards God from all eternity to all eternity.

Learn well this Tablet, O Aḥmad. Chant it during thy days and withhold not thyself therefrom. For verily, God hath ordained for the one who chanteth it, the reward of a hundred martyrs and a service in both worlds. These favors have We bestowed upon thee as a bounty on Our part and a mercy from Our presence, that thou mayest be of those who are grateful.

By God! Should one who is in affliction or grief read this Tablet with absolute sincerity,

God will dispel his sadness, solve his difficulties and remove his afflictions.

Verily, He is the Merciful, the Compassionate. Praise be to God, the Lord of all the worlds.

— *Bahá'u'lláh*

FIRE TABLET

In the Name of God, the Most Ancient, the Most Great.

Indeed the hearts of the sincere are consumed in the fire of separation: Where is the gleaming of the light of Thy Countenance, O Beloved of the worlds?

Those who are near unto Thee have been abandoned in the darkness of desolation: Where is the shining of the morn of Thy reunion, O Desire of the worlds?

The bodies of Thy chosen ones lie quivering on distant sands: Where is the ocean of Thy presence, O Enchanter of the worlds?

Longing hands are uplifted to the heaven of Thy grace and generosity: Where are the rains of Thy bestowal, O Answerer of the worlds?

The infidels have arisen in tyranny on every hand: Where is the compelling power of Thine ordaining pen, O Conqueror of the worlds?

The barking of dogs is loud on every side: Where is the lion of the forest of Thy might, O Chastiser of the worlds?

Coldness hath gripped all mankind: Where is the warmth of Thy love, O Fire of the worlds?

Calamity hath reached its height: Where are the signs of Thy succor, O Salvation of the worlds?

Darkness hath enveloped most of the peoples: Where is the brightness of Thy splendor, O Radiance of the worlds?

The necks of men are stretched out in malice: Where are the swords of Thy vengeance, O Destroyer of the worlds?

Abasement hath reached its lowest depth: Where are the emblems of Thy glory, O Glory of the worlds?

Sorrows have afflicted the Revealer of Thy Name, the All-Merciful: Where is the joy of the Dayspring of Thy Revelation, O Delight of the worlds?

Anguish hath befallen all the peoples of the earth: Where are the ensigns of Thy gladness, O Joy of the worlds?

Thou seest the Dawning Place of Thy signs

veiled by evil suggestions: Where are the fingers of Thy might, O Power of the worlds?

Sore thirst hath overcome all men: Where is the river of Thy bounty, O Mercy of the worlds?

Greed hath made captive all mankind: Where are the embodiments of detachment, O Lord of the worlds?

Thou seest this Wronged One lonely in exile: Where are the hosts of the heaven of Thy Command, O Sovereign of the worlds?

I have been forsaken in a foreign land: Where are the emblems of Thy faithfulness, O Trust of the worlds?

The agonies of death have laid hold on all men: Where is the surging of Thine ocean of eternal life, O Life of the worlds?

The whisperings of Satan have been breathed to every creature: Where is the meteor of Thy fire, O Light of the worlds?

The drunkenness of passion hath perverted most of mankind: Where are the daysprings of purity, O Desire of the worlds?

Thou seest this Wronged One veiled in tyranny among the Syrians: Where is the radiance of Thy dawning light, O Light of the worlds?

Thou seest Me forbidden to speak forth: Then from where will spring Thy melodies, O Nightingale of the worlds?

Most of the people are enwrapped in fancy and idle imaginings: Where are the exponents of Thy certitude, O Assurance of the worlds?

Bahá is drowning in a sea of tribulation: Where is the Ark of Thy salvation, O Savior of the worlds?

Thou seest the Dayspring of Thine utterance in the darkness of creation: Where is the sun of the heaven of Thy grace, O Light-Giver of the worlds?

The lamps of truth and purity, of loyalty and honor, have been put out: Where are the signs of Thine avenging wrath, O Mover of the worlds?

Canst Thou see any who have championed Thy Self, or who ponder on what hath befallen Him in the pathway of Thy love? Now doth My pen halt, O Beloved of the worlds.

The branches of the Divine Lote-Tree lie broken by the onrushing gales of destiny: Where are the banners of Thy succor, O Champion of the worlds?

This Face is hidden in the dust of slander:

Where are the breezes of Thy compassion, O Mercy of the worlds?

The robe of sanctity is sullied by the people of deceit: Where is the vesture of Thy holiness, O Adorner of the worlds?

The sea of grace is stilled for what the hands of men have wrought: Where are the waves of Thy bounty, O Desire of the worlds?

The door leading to the Divine Presence is locked through the tyranny of Thy foes: Where is the key of Thy bestowal, O Unlocker of the worlds?

The leaves are yellowed by the poisoning winds of sedition: Where is the downpour of the clouds of Thy bounty, O Giver of the worlds?

The universe is darkened with the dust of sin: Where are the breezes of Thy forgiveness, O Forgiver of the worlds?

This Youth is lonely in a desolate land: Where is the rain of Thy heavenly grace, O Bestower of the worlds?

O Supreme Pen, We have heard Thy most sweet call in the eternal realm: Give Thou ear unto what the Tongue of Grandeur uttereth, O Wronged One of the worlds!

Were it not for the cold, how would the heat of Thy words prevail, O Expounder of the worlds?

Were it not for calamity, how would the sun of Thy patience shine, O Light of the worlds?

Lament not because of the wicked. Thou wert created to bear and endure, O Patience of the worlds.

How sweet was Thy dawning on the horizon of the Covenant among the stirrers of sedition, and Thy yearning after God, O Love of the worlds.

By Thee the banner of independence was planted on the highest peaks, and the sea of bounty surged, O Rapture of the worlds.

By Thine aloneness the Sun of Oneness shone, and by Thy banishment the land of Unity was adorned. Be patient, O Thou Exile of the worlds.

We have made abasement the garment of glory, and affliction the adornment of Thy temple, O Pride of the worlds.

Thou seest the hearts are filled with hate, and to overlook is Thine, O Thou Concealer of the sins of the worlds.

When the swords flash, go forward! When

the shafts fly, press onward! O Thou Sacrifice of the worlds.

Dost Thou wail, or shall I wail? Rather shall I weep at the fewness of Thy champions, O Thou Who hast caused the wailing of the worlds.

Verily, I have heard Thy Call, O All-Glorious Beloved; and now is the face of Bahá flaming with the heat of tribulation and with the fire of Thy shining word, and He hath risen up in faithfulness at the place of sacrifice, looking toward Thy pleasure, O Ordainer of the worlds.

O 'Alí-Akbar, thank thy Lord for this Tablet whence thou canst breathe the fragrance of My meekness, and know what hath beset Us in the path of God, the Adored of all the worlds.

Should all the servants read and ponder this, there shall be kindled in their veins a fire that shall set aflame the worlds.   —*Bahá'u'lláh*

TABLET OF THE HOLY MARINER

"Study the Tablet of the Holy Mariner that ye may know the truth, and consider that the Blessed Beauty hath fully foretold future events. Let them who perceive, take warning."
—'Abdu'l-Bahá

He is the Gracious, the Well-Beloved!
O Holy Mariner!
Bid thine ark of eternity appear before the Celestial Concourse,
   Glorified be my Lord, the All-Glorious!
Launch it upon the ancient sea, in His Name, the Most Wondrous,
   Glorified be my Lord, the All-Glorious!
And let the angelic spirits enter, in the Name of God, the Most High.
   Glorified be my Lord, the All-Glorious!
Unmoor it, then, that it may sail upon the ocean of glory,
   Glorified be my Lord, the All-Glorious!

Haply the dwellers therein may attain the retreats of nearness in the everlasting realm.

Glorified be my Lord, the All-Glorious!

Having reached the sacred strand, the shore of the crimson seas,

Glorified be my Lord, the All-Glorious!

Bid them issue forth and attain this ethereal invisible station,

Glorified be my Lord, the All-Glorious!

A station wherein the Lord hath in the Flame of His Beauty appeared within the deathless tree;

Glorified be my Lord, the All-Glorious!

Wherein the embodiments of His Cause cleansed themselves of self and passion;

Glorified be my Lord, the All-Glorious!

Around which the Glory of Moses doth circle with the everlasting hosts;

Glorified be my Lord, the All-Glorious!

Wherein the Hand of God was drawn forth from His bosom of Grandeur;

Glorified be my Lord, the All-Glorious!

Wherein the ark of the Cause remaineth motionless even though to its dwellers be declared all divine attributes.

Glorified be my Lord, the All-Glorious!
O Mariner! Teach them that are within the ark
that which we have taught thee behind the mystic veil.

Glorified be my Lord, the All-Glorious!
Perchance they may not tarry in the sacred
snow-white spot,

Glorified be my Lord, the All-Glorious!
But may soar upon the wings of the spirit unto
that station which the Lord hath exalted above
all mention in the worlds below,

Glorified be my Lord, the All-Glorious!
May wing through space even as the favored
birds in the realm of eternal reunion;

Glorified be my Lord, the All-Glorious!
May know the mysteries hidden in the Seas of
light.

Glorified be my Lord, the All-Glorious!
They passed the grades of worldly limitations
and reached that of the divine unity, the center of heavenly guidance.

Glorified be my Lord, the All-Glorious!
They have desired to ascend unto that state
which the Lord hath ordained to be above their
stations.

Glorified be my Lord, the All-Glorious!
Whereupon the burning meteor cast them out
from them that abide in the Kingdom of His
Presence,

Glorified be my Lord, the All-Glorious!
And they heard the Voice of Grandeur raised
from behind the unseen pavilion upon the
Height of Glory:

Glorified be my Lord, the All-Glorious!
"O guardian angels! Return them to their abode
in the world below,

Glorified be my Lord, the All-Glorious!
"Inasmuch as they have purposed to rise to that
sphere which the wings of the celestial dove
have never attained;

Glorified be my Lord, the All-Glorious!
"Whereupon the ship of fancy standeth still
which the minds of them that comprehend
cannot grasp."

Glorified be my Lord, the All-Glorious!
Whereupon the maid of heaven looked out
from her exalted chamber,

Glorified be my Lord, the All-Glorious!
And with her brow signed to the Celestial Concourse,

Glorified be my Lord, the All-Glorious!
Flooding with the light of her countenance the heaven and the earth,

Glorified be my Lord, the All-Glorious!
And as the radiance of her beauty shone upon the people of dust,

Glorified be my Lord, the All-Glorious!
All beings were shaken in their mortal graves.

Glorified be my Lord, the All-Glorious!
She then raised the call which no ear through all eternity hath ever heard,

Glorified be my Lord, the All-Glorious!
And thus proclaimed: "By the Lord! He whose heart hath not the fragrance of the love of the exalted and glorious Arabian Youth,

Glorified be my Lord, the All-Glorious!
"Can in no wise ascend unto the glory of the highest heaven."

Glorified be my Lord, the All-Glorious!
Thereupon she summoned unto herself one maiden from her handmaidens,

Glorified be my Lord, the All-Glorious!
And commanded her: "Descend into space from the mansions of eternity,

Glorified be my Lord, the All-Glorious!

"And turn thou unto that which they have concealed in the inmost of their hearts.

Glorified be my Lord, the All-Glorious!
"Shouldst thou inhale the perfume of the robe from the Youth that hath been hidden within the tabernacle of light by reason of that which the hands of the wicked have wrought,

Glorified be my Lord, the All-Glorious!
"Raise a cry within thyself, that all the inmates of the chambers of Paradise, that are the embodiments of the eternal wealth, may understand and hearken;

Glorified be my Lord, the All-Glorious!
"That they may all come down from their everlasting chambers and tremble,

Glorified be my Lord, the All-Glorious!
"And kiss their hands and feet for having soared to the heights of faithfulness;

Glorified be my Lord, the All-Glorious!
"Perchance they may find from their robes the fragrance of the Beloved One."

Glorified be my Lord, the All-Glorious!
Thereupon the countenance of the favored damsel beamed above the celestial chambers even as the light that shineth from the face of the Youth above His mortal temple;

Glorified be my Lord, the All-Glorious!
She then descended with such an adorning as
to illumine the heavens and all that is therein.

Glorified be my Lord, the All-Glorious!
She bestirred herself and perfumed all things
in the lands of holiness and grandeur.

Glorified be my Lord, the All-Glorious!
When she reached that place she rose to her
full height in the midmost heart of creation,

Glorified be my Lord, the all-Glorious!
And sought to inhale their fragrance at a time
that knoweth neither beginning nor end.

Glorified be my Lord, the All-Glorious!
She found not in them that which she did desire, and this, verily, is but one of His wondrous tales.

Glorified be my Lord, the All-Glorious!
She then cried aloud, wailed and repaired to
her own station within her most lofty mansion,

Glorified be my Lord, the All-Glorious!
And then gave utterance to one mystic word,
whispered privily by her honeyed tongue,

Glorified be my Lord, the All-Glorious!
And raised the call amidst the Celestial Concourse and the immortal maids of heaven:

Glorified be my Lord, the All-Glorious!

"By the Lord! I found not from these idle claimants the breeze of Faithfulness!

Glorified be my Lord, the All-Glorious!
"By the Lord! The Youth hath remained lone and forlorn in the land of exile in the hands of the ungodly."

Glorified be my Lord, the All-Glorious!
She then uttered within herself such a cry that the Celestial Concourse did shriek and tremble,

Glorified be my Lord, the All-Glorious!
And she fell upon the dust and gave up the spirit. It seemeth she was called and hearkened unto Him that summoned her unto the Realm on High.

Glorified be my Lord, the All-Glorious!
Glorified be He that created her out of the essence of love in the midmost heart of His exalted paradise!

Glorified be my Lord, the All-Glorious!
Thereupon the maids of heaven hastened forth from their chambers, upon whose countenances the eye of no dweller in the highest paradise had ever gazed.

Glorified be our Lord, the Most High!
They all gathered around her, and lo! they found her body fallen upon the dust;

Glorified be our Lord, the Most High!
And as they beheld her state and comprehended
a word of the tale told by the Youth, they bared
their heads, rent their garments asunder, beat
upon their faces, forgot their joy, shed tears and
smote with their hands upon their cheeks, and
this is verily one of the mysterious grievous
afflictions—
Glorified be our Lord, the Most High!

—*Bahá'u'lláh*

TABLETS OF VISITATION

(This Tablet is read at the Shrines of Bahá'u'lláh and the Báb. It is also frequently used in commemorating Their anniversaries.)

The praise which hath dawned from Thy most august Self, and the glory which hath shone forth from Thy most effulgent Beauty, rest upon Thee, O Thou Who art the Manifestation of Grandeur, and the King of Eternity, and the Lord of all who are in heaven and on earth! I testify that through Thee the sovereignty of God and His dominion, and the majesty of God and His grandeur, were revealed, and the Daystars of ancient splendor have shed their radiance in the heaven of Thine irrevocable decree, and the Beauty of the Unseen hath shone forth above the horizon of creation. I testify, moreover, that with but a movement of Thy Pen Thine injunction "Be Thou" hath been enforced, and God's hidden Secret hath been divulged, and all created things have been called into being, and all the Revelations have been sent down.

I bear witness, moreover, that through Thy beauty the beauty of the Adored One hath been unveiled, and through Thy face the face of the Desired One hath shone forth, and that through a word from Thee Thou hast decided between all created things, causing them who are devoted to Thee to ascend unto the summit of glory, and the infidels to fall into the lowest abyss.

I bear witness that he who hath known Thee hath known God, and he who hath attained unto Thy presence hath attained unto the presence of God. Great, therefore, is the blessedness of him who hath believed in Thee, and in Thy signs, and hath humbled himself before Thy sovereignty, and hath been honored with meeting Thee, and hath attained the good pleasure of Thy will, and circled around Thee, and stood before Thy throne. Woe betide him that hath transgressed against Thee, and hath denied Thee, and repudiated Thy signs, and gainsaid Thy sovereignty, and risen up against Thee, and waxed proud before Thy face, and hath disputed Thy testimonies, and fled from Thy rule and Thy dominion, and been numbered with the infidels whose names have been inscribed by the fingers of Thy behest upon Thy holy Tablets.

Waft, then, unto me, O my God and my Beloved, from the right hand of Thy mercy and Thy loving-kindness, the holy breaths of Thy favors, that they may draw me away from myself and from the world unto the courts of Thy nearness and Thy presence. Potent art Thou to do what pleaseth Thee. Thou, truly, hast been supreme over all things.

The remembrance of God and His praise, and the glory of God and His splendor, rest upon Thee, O Thou Who art His Beauty! I bear witness that the eye of creation hath never gazed upon one wronged like Thee. Thou wast immersed all the days of Thy life beneath an ocean of tribulations. At one time Thou wast in chains and fetters; at another Thou wast threatened by the sword of Thine enemies. Yet, despite all this, Thou didst enjoin upon all men to observe what had been prescribed unto Thee by Him Who is the All-Knowing, the All-Wise.

May my spirit be a sacrifice to the wrongs Thou didst suffer, and my soul be a ransom for the adversities Thou didst sustain. I beseech God, by Thee and by them whose faces have been illumined with the splendors of the light of Thy countenance, and who, for love of Thee, have observed all whereunto they were bidden, to remove the veils that have come in between Thee and Thy creatures, and to supply me with the good of this world and the world to come. Thou art, in truth, the Almighty, the Most Exalted, the All-Glorious, the Ever-Forgiving, the Most Compassionate.

Bless Thou, O Lord my God, the Divine Lote-Tree and its leaves, and its boughs, and its branches, and its stems, and its offshoots, as long as Thy most excellent titles will endure and Thy most august attributes will last. Protect it, then, from the mischief of the aggressor and the hosts of tyranny. Thou art, in truth, the Almighty, the Most Powerful. Bless Thou, also, O Lord my God, Thy servants and Thy handmaidens who have attained unto Thee.

Thou, truly, art the All-Bountiful, Whose grace is infinite. No God is there save Thee, the Ever-Forgiving, the Most Generous.   —*Bahá'u'lláh*

(This prayer, revealed by 'Abdu'l-Bahá, is read at His Shrine. It is also used in private prayer.)

Whoso reciteth this prayer with lowliness and fervor will bring gladness and joy to the heart of this Servant; it will be even as meeting Him face to face.

He is the All-Glorious!

O God, my God! Lowly and tearful, I raise my suppliant hands to Thee and cover my face in the dust of that Threshold of Thine, exalted above the knowledge of the learned, and the praise of all that glorify Thee. Graciously look upon Thy servant, humble and lowly at Thy door, with the glances of the eye of Thy mercy, and immerse him in the Ocean of Thine eternal grace.

Lord! He is a poor and lowly servant of Thine, enthralled and imploring Thee, captive in Thy hand, praying fervently to Thee, trusting in Thee, in tears before Thy face, calling to Thee and beseeching Thee, saying:

O Lord, my God! Give me Thy grace to serve Thy loved ones, strengthen me in my servitude to Thee, illumine my brow with the light of adoration in Thy court of holiness, and of prayer to Thy kingdom of grandeur. Help me to be selfless at the heavenly entrance of Thy gate, and aid me to be detached from all things within Thy holy precincts. Lord! Give me to drink from the chalice of selflessness; with its robe clothe me, and in its ocean immerse me. Make me as dust in the pathway of Thy loved ones, and grant that I may offer up my soul for the earth ennobled by the footsteps of Thy chosen ones in Thy path, O Lord of Glory in the Highest.

With this prayer doth Thy servant call Thee, at dawntide and in the night-season. Fulfill his heart's desire, O Lord! Illumine his heart, gladden his bosom, kindle his light, that he may serve Thy Cause and Thy servants.

Thou art the Bestower, the Pitiful, the Most Bountiful, the Gracious, the Merciful, the Compassionate.
— 'Abdu'l-Bahá

ALPHABETICAL INDEX
TO FIRST LINES OF PRAYERS

The first lines of prayers revealed by Bahá'u'lláh and the Báb are in italics, those by 'Abdu'l-Bahá are in roman type.